FOCUS POCUS

90-DAY GUIDED JOURNAL

CREATIVE REFLECTIONS for INTENTION and MINDFULNESS

KIMOTHY JOY

Andrews McMeel
PUBLISHING®

Andrews McMeel Publishing
a division of Andrews McMeel Universal
1130 Walnut Street, Kansas City, Missouri 64106

www.andrewsmcmeel.com

23 24 25 26 27 RLP 10 9 8 7 6 5 4 3 2 1

ISBN: 978-1-5248-7875-7

Editor: Jono Jarrett
Art Director/Designer: Jenny Mohrfeld
Production Editor: Elizabeth A. Garcia
Production Manager: Chuck Harper

ATTENTION: SCHOOLS AND BUSINESSES
Andrews McMeel books are available at quantity discounts with bulk purchase for educational, business, or sales promotional use. For information, please e-mail the Andrews McMeel Publishing Special Sales Department: sales@amuniversal.com.

Growing up, I was never taught how to cope with life, to be mindful or intentional, or how to love myself. I wasn't taught to listen to my inner knowing before asking the outside world for answers. My goals were as scattered as my thoughts and mainly influenced by my parents, friends, church, society, and the media.

At 30, I stopped running from myself for once and started spending time alone, painting with watercolors daily. It became therapy and a gateway back into my heart: I started to hear my own inner wisdom more clearly. From there, I discovered different pathways to access my soul. I started meditating, writing gratitude lists, setting intentions, experimenting with manifesting, and working with therapists, shamans, mediums, astrologists, women's circles, and many more. I was excavating to get to know my true self, and it wasn't always pretty. It was often painful and confronting yet beyond rewarding.

Desiring a consistent way to check in with my heart and the Universe, I played with different journaling exercises consisting of my favorite mindfulness techniques until I came up with one that helped me honor my true feelings, calm the chaotic chatter, and create a strong intention, or focus, for the day. It was brief but had depth. I made my own template, one that was hand-painted and hand-lettered, visually lush, and creative. This 15-minute practice was jam-packed with goodness and results.

Magic unfolded. So did healing and clarity. I felt more grounded and connected to myself, my desires, and the Universe on a daily basis. It transformed me.

As I focused on specific things, feelings, and experiences, I observed, often in sheer delight, what transpired. Sometimes what I wrote down would come true in exact detail. I asked for money, and money flowed in. Other times, when I was vague, something greater than I could have imagined would happen. I'd wish for a new, fun, adventurous project, and a surprise invitation to collaborate would land in my inbox. I asked to be reminded of how beautiful and kind people are, and my day would be full of generous interactions with loved ones and strangers. Once, a friend messaged me the exact affirmation I'd written down that morning, word for word, without knowing that was my focus for the day. I was shocked by these synchronicities and by how often they happened, yet soon they became normal. And—get this—the more I showed up honestly and authentically and didn't bypass my true feelings and desires, the more powerful my manifestations became. I highly recommend coupling this practice with healing modalities such as therapy.

THE DEEPER I GO, THE HIGHER I FLOW.

This was too good to not share. If you're reading this, you may be looking for some clarity and calm and maybe even some magic. You're in the right place. This Focus Pocus practice consists of daily journaling and reflection in a framework of twelve open-ended prompts that include proven mindfulness techniques, such as gratitude list making, compassionate self-talk, honoring your authentic emotions, releasing limiting behaviors and thoughts, intention setting, visualization, and inspired action. The prompts guide you through clearing and releasing to the exciting part, creating! Each day's practice culminates in choosing one potent word or affirmation to focus on.

WHERE MY ATTENTION GOES, ENERGY FLOWS, WHAT I FOCUS ON GROWS.

Perhaps you're aware of how powerful it is to have a clear understanding of yourself and your desires—which, by the way, can change from day to day. When we are strongly rooted in who we are and what we want, we're less likely to become overwhelmed by external dramas. It's easier to stay energized and focused on what makes us come alive. And believe me, that is what the world needs! This doesn't mean you tune out the world around you. It means you fill your cup first so it can then pour into others'. Learn to stop letting your attention and energy leak and spill in all directions. Instead, focus it, then let it flow in the direction of your choice. When we are calm and focused, we are more effective humans. We know when to rest and when to take inspired action. Can you imagine what the world would be like if everyone practiced self-compassion and mindfulness, and intentionally used their gifts, talents, and resources to live their highest joy and be of highest service to the world? This is the world I want to create with you.

DON'T LeT your eNeRGY Leak...

Focus iT, then LeT iT flow iN the DiReCTioN of your CHoiCe

To get started, take some time with the introductory pages to set up a solid foundation. Clear your mind through freewriting, then create your ultimate life vision or mood board. Let this be your North Star during the 90-day journey, representing your heart's biggest goals and truest desires. Do not hold back!

Spend 15 to 20 minutes, preferably in the morning, responding to the daily prompts in stillness and presence. This will set your energy for the day. Make sure you're uninterrupted. Try listening to meditation music, whatever gets you into the right headspace. The whole point of this is to feel really, really good and gain clarity from each journaling session. Don't be hard on yourself if you miss a day but make yourself proud by doing what it takes to show up again as soon as you can. Hopefully, this will become one of the best parts of your day, one you won't want to miss!

Here's how the daily ritual works. The beginning prompts help you get into a state of gratitude. From there, you can start to speak more gently to yourself. Next, acknowledge your body and all it does for you (something we often criticize or overlook). Then, name your true feelings without resisting or suppressing them. Choose to feel them fully; then, when you're ready, let them pass through you like clouds in the sky. This loosens their grip on you.

After clearing, it's time to start creating. This is a profound moment to ask your heart and the Universe what it wants you to know right now. Sometimes, you'll hear a very specific desire calling you. ("IT's Time To sTaRT a New CaReeR.") Other times, you will crave a certain emotion. ("ToDay, I NeeD fUN aND aDVeNTURe!") When you bring openness and humility to this process, the Universe will often show you something you didn't even know you wanted or needed. Importantly, don't attempt to micromanage or fixate, and don't expect things to work according to your time line. Don't try to control or manipulate others. Your job is to listen deeply, declare it, and leave it up to the Universe to do the rest. Let the Universe out-dream you!

Once you've written out your requests and desires, take time to visualize them coming true for you. Keep it loose and have fun. Use all your senses and get in the flow. Feel the juicy emotions of it. Don't skip this powerful step. If you feel some doubt or hesitancy come up, make note of that. Get curious about it.

To galvanize your daily practice, declare an affirmation or word as your focal point that captures today's responses. An affirmation is a short, powerful statement that declares a belief you want to claim for yourself; many begin with "I am . . ." Affirmations are potent when repeated and can help override negative or self-sabotaging thoughts. Look at it as your heart telling your ego,

"I believe this to be true no matter what doubt or fear you may throw at me." Revisit your word or affirmation throughout the day whenever you need to recalibrate. Lastly, move your intention out into the world by committing to taking one inspired action in the direction of your dream. Above all, be real. Maybe your inspired action is to take a nap. That is perfect.

For extra potency, there are special pages for each Full Moon and New Moon during each 30-day cycle to help you create rituals that amplify your intentions. After each 30 days, you'll find check-in pages that offer new prompts to reflect, celebrate, clear and release, and create before beginning the next cycle.

While this process builds upon the law of attraction, it takes it a step further. It invites you to show up authentically, look at your shadow aspects, and be willing to be guided by the Universe. It asks that we exercise our manifestation abilities compassionately, responsibly, and with the greater good in mind. I promise you, it's better this way.

This ritual is repetitive on purpose. Oftentimes, we select our goals just with our mind. The repetition will help you hear consistently what your heart and the Universe want for you. You will start to think differently. You'll feel more appreciation for the good within and all around you, be more kind to yourself, and focus on the beauty you are creating in the world. A key ingredient is to believe you are actually worthy of your dreams, a notion that can come with more self-compassion and practice. You might be thinking 90 days is a long time. Is creating a life you love worth it? Is getting to know yourself better and shifting into a more loving, peaceful mindset worth it? Are *you* worth it? Hell, yes! Plus, science tells us it takes at least 66 days on average to form a new habit or way of thinking, so commit wholeheartedly to locking in this new mindset for three months. Perhaps you'll do it every year or with other accountability buddies and focus friends.

MOON MAGIC

New MOON RITUAL

The New Moon is potent for amplifying intentions. It's known to be a time of beginnings and ripe for planting seeds, such as starting new projects, embarking on relationships, and opening ourselves up to new opportunities. Your rituals can be as simple or elaborate as you'd like them to be. You can do the same ones each month or create a new one each time.

Start by creating a calm, sacred space. Next, think about your overarching intention for the 30-day cycle and what you'd like to invite into your life. Focus on how you want to feel. Declare that intention on paper or aloud. Once your intention is declared, take physical action that symbolizes this desire or dream (see below). Finally, release and surrender your request to the Universe. Ask that it be done for your highest good and for the good of others.

New MOON RITUAL activities:

MEDITATE OR PRAY

JOURNAL, DRAW, OR PAINT

CHOREOGRAPH AND/OR PERFORM a DANCE

WRITE AND SING a SONG OR PLAy music

CREATE aN EARTH aLTAR OUTSIDE

GO ON a mINDFUL WALK OR HiKE

SWIM iN NATURAL WATERS

FULL MOON RiTUAL

As we invite new possibilities into our lives, we must also practice letting go. The time during the Full Moon is ripe for releasing and clearing what no longer serves us so that we may make space for what does.

Make a list of everything you're ready to let go of or heal. In a second list, write out what you are inviting in to replace the first list. Place the first list into a fire (safely) or a bowl of water, then watch it dissolve and disappear, just like the old habits, behaviors, and beliefs you are releasing. Once the list is gone, cleanse and renew yourself with a walk in the moonlight, a hot bath in saltwater, or any rejuvenating ritual.

AFFiRMaTiONS

I LiVe iN a WORLD of MAGiC and MiRaCLeS.

I see the BEST iN MYSeLf.
I see the BeST iN everYone I KNOW and iN everYone I MeeT.

WHeN I LiVe mY HiGHeST JOY, I AM iN HiGHeST SeRViCe to the WORLD.

I AM WORTHY of MY DReAMS and DeSiReS.

ALL is WeLL, ALL is WeLL, ALL is WeLL.

I DO WONDeRFUL WORK iN WONDeRFUL WAYS for WONDeRFUL PAY.

I AM GRATeFUL for THE NOW and the BeST is YeT to come.

I AM eNDLeSS ViTALiTY, eNeRGY, and GOOD HeALTH.

I ReST and SaY NO WHeN I NeeD To.

I AM Ascending

I follow My Happy Heart & I Have A Positive, exalment · BLiss TRANSmutin

WHERE MY ATTENTION GOES, ENERGY flows, WHAT I focus on GROWS.

I WILL EMBRACE THIS NEW THOUGHT, BELIEF, OR HABIT

I ASK MY HEART AND THE UNIVERSE TO GUIDE ME.
TODAY, I AM MANIFESTING THIS (OR SOMETHING BETTER)

NOW, I WILL USE THE POWER OF MY IMAGINATION TO VISUALIZE IT
COMING TRUE. FOR THREE MINUTES, WITH EYES CLOSED, I'LL
EXPERIENCE HOW IT MIGHT LOOK, FEEL, SMELL, TASTE, AND SOUND
AS IF IT IS HAPPENING TODAY. I WILL HAVE FUN DAYDREAMING
FREELY AND WON'T GET ATTACHED TO SPECIFIC OUTCOMES.

NOTES FROM MY VISUALIZATION

TO KEEP MY DREAM ALIVE, I WILL FOCUS ON THIS WORD
OR AFFIRMATION TODAY

ONE INSPIRED ACTION I WILL TAKE IN THE DIRECTION OF MY DREAM IS

NOW, I SURRENDER and TRUST. AND SO IT IS.

DAILY 👁 FOCUS

Date _____

Take THREE DEEP BREATHS.

IN THIS moment, I am GRATEFUL FOR

MiRACLES AND BLESSINGS I am CELEBRATING (EVEN ONES ON THE WAY)

I am PROUD of myself FOR

ONE THING I appRECIATE ABOUT my BODY is

I acKNOWLEDGE THESE emOTIONS I'm feeLiNG RIGHT NOW

ONE THOUGHT, LiMiTiNG BELief, OR HABiT I WiLL LET GO of is

WHERE MY ATTENTION GOES, ENERGY flows, WHAT I focus on GROWS.

I WILL EMBRACE THIS NEW THOUGHT, BELIEF, OR HABIT

I ASK MY HEART AND THE UNIVERSE TO GUIDE ME.
TODAY, I AM MANIFESTING THIS (OR SOMETHING BETTER)

NOW, I WILL USE THE POWER OF MY IMAGINATION TO VISUALIZE IT
COMING TRUE. FOR THREE MINUTES, WITH EYES CLOSED, I'LL
EXPERIENCE HOW IT MIGHT LOOK, FEEL, SMELL, TASTE, AND SOUND
AS IF IT IS HAPPENING TODAY. I WILL HAVE FUN DAYDREAMING
FREELY AND WON'T GET ATTACHED TO SPECIFIC OUTCOMES.

NOTES FROM MY VISUALIZATION

TO KEEP MY DREAM ALIVE, I WILL FOCUS ON THIS WORD
OR AFFIRMATION TODAY

ONE INSPIRED ACTION I WILL TAKE IN THE DIRECTION OF MY DREAM IS

NOW, I SURRENDER and TRUST. AND SO IT IS.

DAILY 👁 FOCUS

Date _____

Take THREE DEEP BREATHS.

IN THIS moment, I am GRATEFUL FOR

MIRACLES AND BLESSINGS I am CELEBRATING (even ONES ON THE way)

I am PROUD OF myself FOR

ONE THING I APPRECIATE ABOUT my BODY is

I ACKNOWLEDGE THESE emotions I'm feeling RIGHT NOW

ONE THOUGHT, LIMITING BELIEF, OR HABIT I WILL LET GO OF is

WHERE MY ATTENTION GOES, ENERGY flows, WHAT I focus on GROWS.

I WILL EMBRACE THIS NEW THOUGHT, BELIEF, OR HABIT

I ASK MY HEART AND THE UNIVERSE TO GUIDE ME.
TODAY, I AM MANIFESTING THIS (OR SOMETHING BETTER)

NOW, I WILL USE THE POWER OF MY IMAGINATION TO VISUALIZE IT
COMING TRUE. FOR THREE MINUTES, WITH EYES CLOSED, I'LL
EXPERIENCE HOW IT MIGHT LOOK, FEEL, SMELL, TASTE, AND SOUND
AS IF IT IS HAPPENING TODAY. I WILL HAVE FUN DAYDREAMING
FREELY AND WON'T GET ATTACHED TO SPECIFIC OUTCOMES.

NOTES FROM MY VISUALIZATION

TO KEEP MY DREAM ALIVE, I WILL FOCUS ON THIS WORD
OR AFFIRMATION TODAY

ONE INSPIRED ACTION I WILL TAKE IN THE DIRECTION OF MY DREAM IS

NOW, I SURRENDER and TRUST. AND SO IT IS.

DAILY 👁 FOCUS

Date _____

Take THREE DEEP BREATHS.

In THIS moment, I am GRATEFUL FOR

MIRACLES AND BLESSINGS I am CELEBRATING (EVEN ONES ON THE WAY)

I am PROUD OF myself FOR

ONE THING I APPRECIATE ABOUT my BODY is

I ACKNOWLEDGE THESE emOTIONS I'm FEELING RIGHT NOW

ONE THOUGHT, LimiTING BELIEF, OR HABIT I WILL LET GO OF is

WHERE MY ATTENTION GOES, ENERGY flows, WHAT I focus on GROWS.

I WILL EMBRACE THIS NEW THOUGHT, BELIEF, OR HABIT

I ASK MY HEART AND THE UNIVERSE TO GUIDE ME.
TODAY, I AM MANIFESTING THIS (OR SOMETHING BETTER)

NOW, I WILL USE THE POWER OF MY IMAGINATION TO VISUALIZE IT
COMING TRUE. FOR THREE MINUTES, WITH EYES CLOSED, I'LL
EXPERIENCE HOW IT MIGHT LOOK, FEEL, SMELL, TASTE, AND SOUND
AS IF IT IS HAPPENING TODAY. I WILL HAVE FUN DAYDREAMING
FREELY AND WON'T GET ATTACHED TO SPECIFIC OUTCOMES.

NOTES FROM MY VISUALIZATION

TO KEEP MY DREAM ALIVE, I WILL FOCUS ON THIS WORD
OR AFFIRMATION TODAY

ONE INSPIRED ACTION I WILL TAKE IN THE DIRECTION OF MY DREAM IS

NOW, I SURRENDER and TRUST. AND SO IT IS.

DAILY 👁 FOCUS

Date _____

Take THREE DEEP BREATHS.

IN THIS moment, I am GRATEFUL FOR

MIRACLES AND BLESSINGS I am CELEBRATING (EVEN ONES ON THE WAY)

I am PROUD OF myself FOR

ONE THING I APPRECIATE ABOUT my BODY is

I ACKNOWLEDGE THESE emotions I'm FEELING RIGHT NOW

ONE THOUGHT, LIMITING BELIEF, OR HABIT I WILL LET GO OF is

WHere MY ATTeNTioN GoeS, eNerGY flows, WHAT I focuS on GROWS.

I WiLL eMBRaCe THiS NeW THOUGHT, BeLief, OR HaBiT

I aSK my HeaRT aND THe UNiverSe TO GUiDe me.
TODaY, I am maNifeSTiNG THiS (OR SOMeTHiNG BeTTer)

NOW, I WiLL USe THe POWeR of my imaGiNaTioN TO ViSUaLiZe iT
COmiNG TRUe. FOR THRee miNUTeS, WiTH eyeS CLOSeD, I'LL
eXPeRieNCe HOW iT miGHT LOOK, feeL, SmeLL, TaSTe, aND SOUND
aS if iT iS HaPPeNiNG TODaY. I WiLL HaVe fUN DayDReamiNG
fReeLy aND WON'T GeT aTTaCHeD TO SPeCifiC OUTCOmeS.

NOTeS fROm my ViSUaLiZaTioN

TO KeeP my DReam aLiVe, I WiLL fOCUS ON THiS WORD
OR affiRmaTioN TODaY

ONe iNSPiReD aCTioN I WiLL TaKe iN THe DiReCTioN of my DReam iS

NOW, I SURReNDer and TRUST. AND SO iT iS.

DAILY 👁 FOCUS

Date _____

Take THREE DEEP BREATHS.

IN THIS moment, I am GRATEFUL foR

MiRacLES aND BLESSiNGS I am CELEBRATiNG (EVEN ONES ON THE way)

I am PROUD of mySELf foR

ONE THiNG I appReciaTE aBOUT my BODy is

I acKNOWLEDGE THESE emOTiONS I'm fEELiNG RiGHT NOW

ONE THOUGHT, LimiTiNG BELiEf, OR HaBiT I WiLL LET GO of is

WHERE MY ATTENTION GOES, ENERGY flows, WHAT I focus on GROWS.

I WILL EMBRACE THIS NEW THOUGHT, BELIEF, OR HABIT

I ASK my HEART AND THE UNIVERSE TO GUIDE me.
TODAY, I am manifesting THIS (OR SOMETHING BETTER)

NOW, I WILL USE THE POWER of my IMAGINATION TO VISUALIZE IT
COMING TRUE. FOR THREE MINUTES, WITH eyes CLOSED, I'LL
EXPERIENCE HOW IT MIGHT LOOK, feel, SMELL, TASTE, AND SOUND
AS IF IT IS HAPPENING TODAY. I WILL HAVE fUN DAYDREAMING
fREELY AND WON'T GET ATTACHED TO SPECIFIC OUTCOMES.

NOTES fROM my VISUALIZATION

TO KEEP my DREAM ALIVE, I WILL focus ON THIS WORD
OR affIRMATION TODAY

ONE INSPIRED ACTION I WILL TAKE IN THE DIRECTION of my DREAM IS

NOW, I SURRENDER and TRUST. AND SO IT IS.

DAILY 👁 FOCUS

Date _____

Take THReE DeeP BReaTHS.

In THiS moment, I am GRaTeFUL FOR

Miracles and Blessings I am celeBRaTinG (even ones on THe way)

I am PROUD of myself for

One THinG I apPReciaTe aBoUT my BoDY is

I acknowLeDGe THese emOTIONS I'm feelinG RiGHT now

One THOUGHT, Limiting Belief, OR HaBiT I WiLL LeT GO of is

WHERE MY ATTENTION GOES, ENERGY flows, WHAT I focus on GROWS.

I WILL EMBRACE THIS NEW THOUGHT, BELIEF, OR HABIT

I ASK MY HEART AND THE UNIVERSE TO GUIDE ME.
TODAY, I AM MANIFESTING THIS (OR SOMETHING BETTER)

NOW, I WILL USE THE POWER OF MY IMAGINATION TO VISUALIZE IT
COMING TRUE. FOR THREE MINUTES, WITH EYES CLOSED, I'LL
EXPERIENCE HOW IT MIGHT LOOK, FEEL, SMELL, TASTE, AND SOUND
AS IF IT IS HAPPENING TODAY. I WILL HAVE FUN DAYDREAMING
FREELY AND WON'T GET ATTACHED TO SPECIFIC OUTCOMES.

NOTES FROM MY VISUALIZATION

TO KEEP MY DREAM ALIVE, I WILL FOCUS ON THIS WORD
OR AFFIRMATION TODAY

ONE INSPIRED ACTION I WILL TAKE IN THE DIRECTION OF MY DREAM IS

NOW, I SURRENDER and TRUST. AND SO IT IS.

DAILY 👁 FOCUS

Date _____

Take THREE DEEP BREATHS.

In THIS moment, I am GRATEFUL foR

Miracles and BLessings I am CeLeBRating (even ones on the way)

I am PROUD of myself foR

One THING I appReciate aBOUT my BODy is

I acKNOWLeDGe THESe emotions I'm feeLING RIGHT NOW

One THOUGHT, Limiting BeLief, OR HaBiT I WILL Let GO of is

WHERE MY ATTENTION GOES, ENERGY flows, WHAT I focus on GROWS.

I WILL EMBRACE THIS NEW THOUGHT, BELIEF, OR HABIT

I ASK MY HEART AND THE UNIVERSE TO GUIDE ME.
TODAY, I AM MANIFESTING THIS (OR SOMETHING BETTER)

NOW, I WILL USE THE POWER OF MY IMAGINATION TO VISUALIZE IT
COMING TRUE. FOR THREE MINUTES, WITH EYES CLOSED, I'LL
EXPERIENCE HOW IT MIGHT LOOK, FEEL, SMELL, TASTE, AND SOUND
AS IF IT IS HAPPENING TODAY. I WILL HAVE FUN DAYDREAMING
FREELY AND WON'T GET ATTACHED TO SPECIFIC OUTCOMES.

NOTES FROM MY VISUALIZATION

TO KEEP MY DREAM ALIVE, I WILL FOCUS ON THIS WORD
OR AFFIRMATION TODAY

ONE INSPIRED ACTION I WILL TAKE IN THE DIRECTION OF MY DREAM IS

NOW, I SURRENDER and TRUST. AND SO IT IS.

DAILY 👁 FOCUS

Date _____

Take THREE DeeP BReaTHs.

IN THis moment, I am GRaTeFuL FoR

MiRaCLes aND BLessiNGs I am CeLeBRaTiNG (eveN oNes oN THe way)

I am PRouD of myself FoR

oNe THiNG I aPPReCiaTe aBouT my BoDy is

I aCkNowLeDGe THese emoTioNs I'm FeeLiNG RiGHT Now

oNe THouGHT, LimiTiNG BeLieF, oR HaBiT I wiLL LeT Go of is

WHere my ATTeNTioN Goes, eNeRGY flows, WHAT I focus on GROWS.

I WILL emBRace THis New THOUGHT, BeLief, oR HaBiT

I ask my HeaRT aND THe UNiveRse To GUide me.
ToDay, I am manifesTiNG THis (oR someTHiNG BeTTeR)

Now, I WILL Use THe PoweR of my imaGiNaTioN To visuaLize iT
comiNG TRUe. FoR THRee miNUTes, WiTH eyes CLosed, I'LL
expeRieNce HoW iT miGHT LooK, feeL, smeLL, TasTe, aND souND
as if iT is HappeNiNG ToDay. I WILL Have fUN DayDReamiNG
fReeLy aND woN'T GeT aTTacHed To specific ouTcomes.

NoTes fRom my visuaLizaTioN

TO Keep my DReam aLive, I WILL focus oN THis woRD
oR affiRmaTioN ToDay

oNe iNspiRed acTioN I WILL TaKe iN THe DiRecTioN of my DReam is

Now, I SURReNDeR aND TRUST. AND so iT is.

DAILY 👁 FOCUS

Date _____

Take THREE DEEP BREATHS.

IN THIS moment, I am GRATEFUL FOR

MiRaCLeS aND BLeSSiNGS I am CeLeBRaTiNG (even ones on THe way)

I am PROUD of myseLf fOR

ONe THiNG I appReciaTe aBOUT my BODy is

I acKNOWLeDGe THese emoTiONS I'm feeLiNG RiGHT NOW

ONe THOUGHT, LimiTiNG BeLief, OR HaBiT I WiLL LeT GO Of is

WHERE MY ATTENTION GOES, ENERGY flows, WHAT I focus on GROWS.

I WILL EMBRACE THIS NEW THOUGHT, BELIEF, OR HABIT

I ASK MY HEART AND THE UNIVERSE TO GUIDE ME.
TODAY, I AM MANIFESTING THIS (OR SOMETHING BETTER)

NOW, I WILL USE THE POWER OF MY IMAGINATION TO VISUALIZE IT
COMING TRUE. FOR THREE MINUTES, WITH EYES CLOSED, I'LL
EXPERIENCE HOW IT MIGHT LOOK, FEEL, SMELL, TASTE, AND SOUND
AS IF IT IS HAPPENING TODAY. I WILL HAVE FUN DAYDREAMING
FREELY AND WON'T GET ATTACHED TO SPECIFIC OUTCOMES.

NOTES FROM MY VISUALIZATION

TO KEEP MY DREAM ALIVE, I WILL FOCUS ON THIS WORD
OR AFFIRMATION TODAY

ONE INSPIRED ACTION I WILL TAKE IN THE DIRECTION OF MY DREAM IS

NOW, I SURRENDER and TRUST. AND SO IT IS.

DAILY 👁 FOCUS

Date _____

Take THREE DEEP BREATHS.

IN THIS moment, I am GRATEFUL FOR

MiRaCLes AND BLessiNGS I am CeLeBRaTiNG (even ONes ON THe way)

I am PROUD of myself FOR

ONe THING I appReCiaTe aBOUT my BODy is

I acKNOWLeDGe THese emoTiONS I'm feeLiNG RiGHT NOW

ONe THOUGHT, LimiTiNG BeLief, OR HaBiT I WiLL LeT GO of is

WHERE MY ATTENTION GOES, ENERGY flows, WHAT I focus on GROWS.

I WILL EMBRACE THIS NEW THOUGHT, BELIEF, OR HABIT

I ASK MY HEART AND THE UNIVERSE TO GUIDE ME.
TODAY, I AM MANIFESTING THIS (OR SOMETHING BETTER)

NOW, I WILL USE THE POWER OF MY IMAGINATION TO VISUALIZE IT
COMING TRUE. FOR THREE MINUTES, WITH EYES CLOSED, I'LL
EXPERIENCE HOW IT MIGHT LOOK, FEEL, SMELL, TASTE, AND SOUND
AS IF IT IS HAPPENING TODAY. I WILL HAVE FUN DAYDREAMING
FREELY AND WON'T GET ATTACHED TO SPECIFIC OUTCOMES.

NOTES FROM MY VISUALIZATION

TO KEEP MY DREAM ALIVE, I WILL FOCUS ON THIS WORD
OR AFFIRMATION TODAY

ONE INSPIRED ACTION I WILL TAKE IN THE DIRECTION OF MY DREAM IS

NOW, I SURRENDER and TRUST. AND SO IT IS.

DAILY 👁 FOCUS

Date _____

Take THREE DEEP BREATHS.

In THIS moment, I am GRATEFUL FOR

MiRacLes aND BLessiNGS I am CeLeBRaTiNG (even ONes ON THe way)

I am PROUD of myseLf FOR

ONe THiNG I appReciaTe aBOUT my BODy is

I acKNOWLeDGe THese emOTiONS I'm feeLiNG RiGHT NOW

ONe THOUGHT, LimiTiNG BeLief, OR HaBiT I wiLL LeT GO of is

WHERE MY ATTENTION GOES, ENERGY flows, WHAT I focus on GROWS.

I WILL EMBRACE THIS NEW THOUGHT, BELIEF, OR HABIT

I ASK MY HEART AND THE UNIVERSE TO GUIDE ME.
TODAY, I AM MANIFESTING THIS (OR SOMETHING BETTER)

NOW, I WILL USE THE POWER OF MY IMAGINATION TO VISUALIZE IT
COMING TRUE. FOR THREE MINUTES, WITH EYES CLOSED, I'LL
EXPERIENCE HOW IT MIGHT LOOK, FEEL, SMELL, TASTE, AND SOUND
AS IF IT IS HAPPENING TODAY. I WILL HAVE FUN DAYDREAMING
FREELY AND WON'T GET ATTACHED TO SPECIFIC OUTCOMES.

NOTES FROM MY VISUALIZATION

TO KEEP MY DREAM ALIVE, I WILL FOCUS ON THIS WORD
OR AFFIRMATION TODAY

ONE INSPIRED ACTION I WILL TAKE IN THE DIRECTION OF MY DREAM IS

NOW, I SURRENDER and TRUST. AND SO IT IS.

DAILY 👁 FOCUS

Date _____

Take THREE DEEP BREATHS.

IN THIS moment, I am GRATEFUL FOR

MIRACLES AND BLESSINGS I am CELEBRATING (EVEN ONES ON THE WAY)

I am PROUD of myself FOR

ONE THING I appreciate aBOUT my BODY is

I ACKNOWLEDGE THESE emotions I'm feeling RIGHT NOW

ONE THOUGHT, LIMITING BELIEF, OR HABIT I WILL LET GO of is

WHere my ATTeNTioN Goes, eNeRGY flows, WHaT I focus on GROWS.

I WiLL emBRaCe THiS New THOUGHT, BeLief, OR HaBiT

I aSK my HeaRT aND THe UNiVeRSe TO GUiDe me.
TODaY, I am manifeSTiNG THiS (OR SOmeTHiNG BeTTeR)

Now, I WiLL USe THe POWeR of my imaGiNaTiON TO ViSUaLiZe iT
COmiNG TRUe. FOR THRee miNUTeS, WiTH eyeS CLOSeD, I'LL
exPeRieNCe HOW iT miGHT LOOK, feeL, SmeLL, TaSTe, aND SOUND
as if iT iS HaPPeNiNG TODaY. I WiLL HaVe fUN DaYDReamiNG
fReeLY aND WON'T GeT aTTaCHeD TO SPeCifiC OUTCOmeS.

NOTeS fROm my ViSUaLiZaTiON

TO KeeP my DReam aLiVe, I WiLL fOCUS ON THiS WORD
OR affiRmaTiON TODaY

ONe iNSPiReD aCTiON I WiLL TaKe iN THe DiReCTiON of my DReam iS

NOW, I SURReNDer and TRUST. AND SO iT iS.

DAILY 👁 FOCUS

Date _____

Take THREE Deep BREaTHS.

In THiS moment, I am GRaTeFUL FOR

Miracles and BLessiNGS I am CeLeBRaTiNG (even ones on THe way)

I am PROUD of myseLf FOR

One THiNG I aPPReciaTe aBOUT my BODy is

I acKNOWLeDGe THese emoTioNS I'm feeLiNG RiGHT NOW

One THOUGHT, LimiTiNG BeLief, OR HaBiT I WiLL LeT GO of is

WHERE MY ATTENTION GOES, ENERGY flows, WHAT I focus on GROWS.

I WILL EMBRACE THIS NEW THOUGHT, BELIEF, OR HABIT

I ASK MY HEART AND THE UNIVERSE TO GUIDE ME.
TODAY, I AM MANIFESTING THIS (OR SOMETHING BETTER)

NOW, I WILL USE THE POWER OF MY IMAGINATION TO VISUALIZE IT
COMING TRUE. FOR THREE MINUTES, WITH EYES CLOSED, I'LL
EXPERIENCE HOW IT MIGHT LOOK, FEEL, SMELL, TASTE, AND SOUND
AS IF IT IS HAPPENING TODAY. I WILL HAVE FUN DAYDREAMING
FREELY AND WON'T GET ATTACHED TO SPECIFIC OUTCOMES.

NOTES FROM MY VISUALIZATION

TO KEEP MY DREAM ALIVE, I WILL FOCUS ON THIS WORD
OR AFFIRMATION TODAY

ONE INSPIRED ACTION I WILL TAKE IN THE DIRECTION OF MY DREAM IS

NOW, I SURRENDER and TRUST. AND SO IT IS.

DAILY 👁 FOCUS

Date _____

Take three deep breaths.

In this moment, I am grateful for

Miracles and blessings I am celebrating (even ones on the way)

I am proud of myself for

One thing I appreciate about my body is

I acknowledge these emotions I'm feeling right now

One thought, limiting belief, or habit I will let go of is

WHere my ATTeNTioN Goes, eNeRGY flows, WHaT I focus oN GROWS.

I WiLL emBRace THiS New THOUGHT, BeLief, OR HaBiT

I aSK my HeaRT anD THe UNiVeRSe TO GuiDe me.
TODay, I am manifeSTiNG THiS (OR SOmeTHiNG BeTTeR)

NOW, I WiLL USe THe POWeR of my imaGiNATiON TO ViSUaLiZe iT
COmiNG TRUe. FOR THRee miNUTeS, WiTH eyeS CLOSeD, I'LL
eXPeRieNce HOW iT miGHT LOOK, feeL, Smell, TaSTe, anD SOUND
aS if iT iS HaPPeNiNG TODay. I WiLL HaVe fUN DayDReamiNG
fReeLy anD WON'T GeT aTTaCHeD TO SPecific OUTComeS.

NOTeS fROm my ViSUaLiZaTiON

TO KeeP my DReam aLiVe, I WiLL focUS ON THiS WORD
OR affiRmATiON TODay

ONe iNSPiReD aCTiON I WiLL TaKe iN THe DiRecTiON of my DReam iS

NOW, I SURReNDer and TRUST. AND SO iT iS.

DAiLY 👁 FOCUS

Date _____

Take THREE DEEP BREATHS.

In THiS moment, I am GRATEFUL FOR

Miracles and BLESSINGS I am CELEBRATING (even ONES ON THE WAY)

I am PROUD of myself FOR

ONE THING I appreciate aBOUT my BODY is

I acKNOWLEDGE THESE emoTions I'm feeLinG RiGHT NOW

ONE THOUGHT, LimiTinG Belief, OR HaBiT I WILL LET Go of is

WHERE MY ATTENTION GOES, ENERGY flows, WHAT I focus on GROWS.

I WILL EMBRACE THIS NEW THOUGHT, BELIEF, OR HABIT

I ASK my HEART AND THE UNIVERSE TO GUIDE me.
TODAY, I AM manifesting THIS (OR SOMETHING BETTER)

NOW, I WILL USE THE POWER OF my imaGiNATION TO VISUALIZE iT
COMING TRUE. FOR THREE minUTES, WITH eyes CLOSED, I'LL
EXPERIENCE HOW iT MIGHT LOOK, feel, SMELL, TASTE, AND SOUND
AS iF iT iS HAPPENING TODAY. I WILL HAVE fUN DayDREAMING
fREELY AND WON'T GET ATTACHED TO SPECIFIC OUTCOMES.

NOTES fROM my VISUALIZATION

TO KEEP my DREAM aLIVE, I WILL fOCUS ON THIS WORD
OR affiRMATION TODAY

ONE iNSPiRED ACTION I WILL TAKE iN THE DIRECTION Of my DREAM iS

NOW, I SURRENDER and TRUST. AND SO iT iS.

DAILY 👁 FOCUS

Date _____

Take THREE DEEP BREATHS.

In THIS moment, I am GRATEFUL FOR

Miracles and BLESSINGS I am CELEBRATING (even ones on THE way)

I am PROUD of myself FOR

One THING I appreciate aBOUT my BODY is

I acKNOWLEDGE THESE emoTions I'm feeLING RIGHT NOW

One THOUGHT, LimiTING BeLief, OR HaBiT I WiLL LET GO of is

WHERE MY ATTENTION GOES, ENERGY flows, WHAT I focus on GROWS.

I WILL EMBRACE THIS NEW THOUGHT, BELIEF, OR HABIT

I ASK MY HEART AND THE UNIVERSE TO GUIDE ME.
TODAY, I AM MANIFESTING THIS (OR SOMETHING BETTER)

NOW, I WILL USE THE POWER OF MY IMAGINATION TO VISUALIZE IT
COMING TRUE. FOR THREE MINUTES, WITH EYES CLOSED, I'LL
EXPERIENCE HOW IT MIGHT LOOK, FEEL, SMELL, TASTE, AND SOUND
AS IF IT IS HAPPENING TODAY. I WILL HAVE FUN DAYDREAMING
FREELY AND WON'T GET ATTACHED TO SPECIFIC OUTCOMES.

NOTES FROM MY VISUALIZATION

TO KEEP MY DREAM ALIVE, I WILL FOCUS ON THIS WORD
OR AFFIRMATION TODAY

ONE INSPIRED ACTION I WILL TAKE IN THE DIRECTION OF MY DREAM IS

NOW, I SURRENDER and TRUST. AND SO IT IS.

DAILY 👁 FOCUS

Date _____

Take THREE DEEP BREATHS.

IN THIS moment, I am GRATEFUL FOR

MIRACLES AND BLESSINGS I am CELEBRATING (EVEN ONES ON THE WAY)

I am PROUD of myself FOR

ONE THING I APPRECIATE ABOUT my BODY is

I ACKNOWLEDGE THESE emotions I'm FEELING RIGHT NOW

ONE THOUGHT, LIMITING BELIEF, OR HABIT I WILL LET GO of is

WHere my ATTeNTioN Goes, eNeRGY flows, WHaT I focus on GROWS.

I WiLL eMBRaCe THiS New THOUGHT, BeLief, OR HaBiT

I aSK my HeaRT aND THe UNiVeRSe TO GUiDe me.
TODaY, I am manifeSTiNG THiS (OR SOmeTHiNG BeTTeR)

NOW, I WiLL USe THe POWeR of my imaGiNATiON TO ViSUaLize iT
COmiNG TRUe. FOR THRee miNUTeS, WiTH eyes CLOSeD, I'LL
eXPeRieNCe HOW iT miGHT LOOK, feeL, SmeLL, TaSTe, aND SOUND
aS if iT iS HaPPeNiNG TODaY. I WiLL HaVe fUN DayDReamiNG
fReeLY aND WON'T GeT aTTaCHeD TO SPeCific OUTComeS.

NOTeS fROm my ViSUaLizaTiON

TO KeeP my DReam aLiVe, I WiLL foCUS ON THiS WORD
OR affiRmATiON TODaY

ONe iNSPiReD aCTiON I WiLL TaKe iN THe DiReCTiON of my DReam iS

NOW, I SURReNDeR and TRUST. AND SO iT iS.

DAILY 👁 FOCUS

Date _____

Take THREE DEEP BREATHS.

IN THIS moment, I am GRATEFUL FOR

MiRACLES AND BLESSINGS I am CELEBRATING (EVEN ONES ON THE WAY)

I am PROUD of myself FOR

ONE THING I APPRECIATE ABOUT my BODY is

I ACKNOWLEDGE THESE emotions I'm FEELING RIGHT NOW

ONE THOUGHT, LiMiTiNG BELIEF, OR HABIT I WILL LET GO of is

WHERE MY ATTENTION GOES, ENERGY flows, WHAT I focus on GROWS.

I WILL EMBRACE THIS NEW THOUGHT, BELIEF, OR HABIT

I ASK my HEART AND THE UNIVERSE TO GUIDE me.
TODAY, I am manifESTING THIS (OR SOMETHING BETTER)

NOW, I WILL USE THE POWER OF my imaGINATION TO visualize iT
COMING TRUE. FOR THREE minuTES, WITH eyes CLOSED, I'LL
experience HOW iT miGHT LOOK, feeL, SMeLL, TaSTE, and SOUND
as if iT iS HAPPENING TODAY. I WILL HAVE fUN DayDReaming
fReeLy AND WON'T GET aTTached TO SPecific OUTcomes.

NOTES fROm my VISUALIZATION

TO KeeP my DReam aLive, I WILL fOCUS ON THIS WORD
OR affiRMaTION TODAY

ONe inSPIReD aCTION I WILL Take in THE DiRecTION of my DReam is

NOW, I SURReNDer and TRUST. AND SO iT iS.

DAILY 👁 FOCUS

Date _____

Take THREE Deep Breaths.

In this moment, I am grateful for

Miracles and blessings I am celebrating (even ones on the way)

I am proud of myself for

One thing I appreciate about my body is

I acknowledge these emotions I'm feeling right now

One thought, limiting belief, or habit I will let go of is

WHERE MY ATTENTION GOES, ENERGY flows, WHAT I focus on GROWS.

I WILL EMBRACE THIS NEW THOUGHT, BELIEF, OR HABIT

I ASK my HEART AND THE UNIVERSE TO GUIDE me.
TODAY, I AM manifesting THIS (OR SOMETHING BETTER)

NOW, I WILL USE THE POWER of my imaGinaTion TO VISUALIZE iT
COMING TRUE. FOR THREE minuTES, WITH eyes CLOSED, I'LL
eXPERIENCE HOW iT MIGHT LOOK, feel, SMELL, TASTE, AND SOUND
AS if iT IS HAPPENING TODAY. I WILL HAVE fUN DayDREaMinG
fReeLY AND WON'T GET ATTACHED TO SPECIFIC OUTCOMES.

NOTES fROM my VISUALIZATION

TO Keep my DREAM ALIVE, I WILL focUS ON THIS WORD
OR affiRMaTION TODAY

ONE INSPIRED ACTION I WILL TAKE IN THE DIRECTION of my DREAM IS

NOW, I SURRENDER and TRUST. AND SO iT IS.

MOON MAGIC

Use these pages to write, draw, or paint about your moon ritual and what you experience.

NeW MOON RiTUAL

Date _____

FULL MOON RiTUAL

Date _____

30-DAY CHECK-IN

Reflect

WHAT HAS BEEN THE BIGGEST IMPACT OF THIS PRACTICE FOR ME?

WHAT HAVE I LEARNED ABOUT MYSELF AND MY DESIRES?

WHAT DID MY HEART AND THE UNIVERSE TEACH ME?

CLEAR and RELEASE

HAVE I STRUGGLED WITH ANY ASPECT OF THIS PRACTICE? WHY?

AM I BUMPING INTO ANY CONSISTENT, BROADER LIMITING BELIEFS, DOUBTS, OR FEARS WHILE DREAMING AND VISUALIZING? WHERE DO THEY COME FROM?

HOW CAN I GIVE MYSELF ADDITIONAL SUPPORT IN HEALING AND RELEASING LIMITING BELIEFS AND STUCK EMOTIONS?

CELEBRATE

IN THE LAST 30 DAYS, WHAT ARE SOME BEAUTIFUL MOMENTS, BLESSINGS, AND MANIFESTATIONS THAT HAVE OCCURRED?

WHAT ARE SOME MAJOR ASPECTS OF MY LIFE THAT I AM GRATEFUL FOR AND PROUD OF?

WHAT DO I LOVE MOST ABOUT MYSELF?
WHAT DO I LOVE MOST ABOUT MY BODY?

CREATE

WHAT ARE MY GREATEST DREAMS AND DESIRES FOR THE NEXT 30 DAYS?

HOW DO I WANT TO FEEL FOR THE NEXT 30 DAYS?

WHAT AM I LOOKING FORWARD TO IN THE NEXT 30 DAYS?

DAILY 👁 FOCUS

Date _____

Take THREE DEEP BREATHS.

IN THIS moment, I am GRATEFUL FOR

MiRacLes aND BLessiNGS I am CeLeBRatiNG (eveN oNes oN THe way)

I am PROUD of myseLf foR

oNe THiNG I appReciate aBoUT my BODY is

I acKNOWLeDGe THese emoTioNS I'm feeLiNG RiGHT NOW

oNe THOUGHT, LimiTiNG BeLief, OR HaBiT I WiLL LeT Go of is

WHERE MY ATTENTION GOES, ENERGY FLOWS, WHAT I FOCUS ON GROWS.

I WILL EMBRACE THIS NEW THOUGHT, BELIEF, OR HABIT

I ASK MY HEART AND THE UNIVERSE TO GUIDE ME.
TODAY, I AM MANIFESTING THIS (OR SOMETHING BETTER)

NOW, I WILL USE THE POWER OF MY IMAGINATION TO VISUALIZE IT
COMING TRUE. FOR THREE MINUTES, WITH EYES CLOSED, I'LL
EXPERIENCE HOW IT MIGHT LOOK, FEEL, SMELL, TASTE, AND SOUND
AS IF IT IS HAPPENING TODAY. I WILL HAVE FUN DAYDREAMING
FREELY AND WON'T GET ATTACHED TO SPECIFIC OUTCOMES.

NOTES FROM MY VISUALIZATION

TO KEEP MY DREAM ALIVE, I WILL FOCUS ON THIS WORD
OR AFFIRMATION TODAY

ONE INSPIRED ACTION I WILL TAKE IN THE DIRECTION OF MY DREAM IS

NOW, I SURRENDER and TRUST. AND SO IT IS.

DAILY 👁 FOCUS

Date _____

Take THREE DeeP BReaTHS.

IN THiS moment, I am GRATefUL foR

MiRaCLeS aND BLeSSiNGS I am CeLeBRaTiNG (even oNeS oN THe way)

I am PROUD of myseLf foR

oNe THiNG I aPPReCiaTe aBOUT my BODy iS

I aCKNOWLeDGe THeSe emoTioNS I'm feeLiNG RiGHT NOW

oNe THOUGHT, LimiTiNG BeLief, oR HaBiT I WiLL LeT Go of iS

WHERE MY ATTENTION GOES, ENERGY flows, WHAT I focus on GROWS.

I WILL EMBRACE THIS NEW THOUGHT, BELIEF, OR HABIT

I ASK MY HEART AND THE UNIVERSE TO GUIDE ME.
TODAY, I AM MANIFESTING THIS (OR SOMETHING BETTER)

NOW, I WILL USE THE POWER OF MY IMAGINATION TO VISUALIZE IT COMING TRUE. FOR THREE MINUTES, WITH EYES CLOSED, I'LL EXPERIENCE HOW IT MIGHT LOOK, FEEL, SMELL, TASTE, AND SOUND AS IF IT IS HAPPENING TODAY. I WILL HAVE FUN DAYDREAMING FREELY AND WON'T GET ATTACHED TO SPECIFIC OUTCOMES.

NOTES FROM MY VISUALIZATION

TO KEEP MY DREAM ALIVE, I WILL FOCUS ON THIS WORD OR AFFIRMATION TODAY

ONE INSPIRED ACTION I WILL TAKE IN THE DIRECTION OF MY DREAM IS

NOW, I SURRENDER AND TRUST. AND SO IT IS.

DAILY 👁 FOCUS

Date _____

Take THREE DEEP BREaTHS.

In THiS moment, I am GRaTefuL foR

MiRaCLeS aND BLeSSiNGS I am CeLeBRaTiNG (eVeN ONeS ON THe Way)

I am PROUD of myseLf foR

ONe THiNG I appReCiaTe aBOUT my BODy is

I aCKNOWLeDGe THeSe emoTiONS I'm feeLiNG RiGHT NOW

ONe THOUGHT, LimiTiNG BeLief, OR HaBiT I WiLL LeT GO of is

WHere MY ATTeNTioN Goes, eNERGY flows, WHAT I focus on GROWS.

I WiLL emBRaCe THiS NeW THOUGHT, BeLief, OR HaBiT

I aSK my HeaRT aND THe UNiVeRSe TO GUiDe me.
TODay, I am manifeSTiNG THiS (OR SOmeTHiNG BeTTeR)

NOW, I WiLL USe THe POWeR of my imaGiNaTiON TO viSUaLize iT
COmiNG TRUe. FOR THRee minUTeS, WiTH eyeS CLOSeD, I'LL
eXPeRieNCe HOW iT miGHT LOOK, feeL, SmeLL, TaSTe, aND SOUND
aS if iT iS HaPPeNiNG TODay. I WiLL HaVe fUN DayDReamiNG
fReeLy aND WON'T GeT aTTaCHeD TO SPeCific OUTCOmeS.

NOTeS fROm my ViSUaLizaTiON

TO KeeP my DReam aLive, I WiLL focUS ON THiS WORD
OR affiRmaTiON TODay

ONe iNSPiReD aCTiON I WiLL TaKe iN THe DiReCTiON of my DReam iS

NOW, I SURReNDer aND TRUST. aND SO iT iS.

DAILY 👁 FOCUS

Date _____

Take THREE DeeP BReaths.

IN THiS moment, I am GRateful foR

Miracles and BLessiNGS I am CeleBRatiNG (even ONes ON The way)

I am PROUD of myself foR

ONe THiNG I appReciate aBOUT my BODY is

I acKNOWLeDGe THese emotioNS I'm feeliNG RiGHT NOW

ONe THOUGHT, Limiting Belief, OR HaBiT I WiLL LeT GO of is

WHERE MY ATTENTION GOES, ENERGY flows, WHAT I focus on GROWS.

I WILL EMBRACE THIS NEW THOUGHT, BELIEF, OR HABIT

I ASK my HEART AND THE UNIVERSE TO GUIDE me.
TODAY, I AM MANIFESTING THIS (OR SOMETHING BETTER)

NOW, I WILL USE THE POWER OF my IMAGINATION TO VISUALIZE IT
COMING TRUE. FOR THREE MINUTES, WITH eyes CLOSED, I'LL
EXPERIENCE HOW IT MIGHT LOOK, feel, SMELL, TASTE, AND SOUND
AS IF IT IS HAPPENING TODAY. I WILL HAVE fUN DAYDREAMING
FREELY AND WON'T GET ATTACHED TO SPECIFIC OUTCOMES.

NOTES FROM my VISUALIZATION

TO KEEP my DREAM ALIVE, I WILL focus ON THIS WORD
OR AFFIRMATION TODAY

ONE INSPIRED ACTION I WILL TAKE IN THE DIRECTION OF my DREAM IS

NOW, I SURRENDER and TRUST. AND SO IT IS.

DAILY 👁 FOCUS

Date _____

Take THREe DeeP BReaTHS.

IN THiS moment, I am GRaTefuL foR

MiRacLes aND BLeSSiNGS I am CeLeBRaTiNG (eveN oNes oN THe way)

I am PROUD of myself foR

oNe THiNG I appReciaTe aBouT my BoDy iS

I acKNowLeDGe THese emoTioNS I'm feeLiNG RiGHT Now

oNe THouGHT, LimiTiNG BeLief, oR HaBiT I wiLL LeT Go of iS

WHERE MY ATTENTION GOES, ENERGY flows, WHAT I focus on GROWS.

I WILL EMBRACE THIS NEW THOUGHT, BELIEF, OR HABIT

I ASK my HEART AND THE UNIVERSE TO GUIDE me.
TODAY, I am manifesting THIS (OR SOMETHING BETTER)

NOW, I WILL USE THE POWER of my imagination TO VISUALIZE IT
COMING TRUE. FOR THREE minutes, WITH eyes CLOSED, I'LL
EXPERIENCE HOW IT MIGHT LOOK, feel, SMELL, TASTE, AND SOUND
AS IF IT IS HAPPENING TODAY. I WILL HAVE FUN DAYDREAMING
fREELY AND WON'T GET ATTACHED TO SPECIFIC OUTCOMES.

NOTES fROM my VISUALIZATION

TO KEEP my DREAM ALIVE, I WILL fOCUS ON THIS WORD
OR affIRMATION TODAY

ONE INSPIRED ACTION I WILL TAKE IN THE DIRECTION of my DREAM IS

NOW, I SURRENDER and TRUST. AND SO IT IS.

DAILY 👁 FOCUS

Date _____

Take THREE DEEP BREATHS.

In THIS moment, I am GRATEFUL FOR

Miracles and BLESSINGS I am CELEBRATING (even ones on the way)

I am PROUD of myself FOR

One THING I appreciate about my BODY is

I acknowledge These emotions I'm feeling RIGHT NOW

One THOUGHT, Limiting Belief, OR HaBiT I WILL LET GO of is

WHere MY ATTeNTioN Goes, eNeRGY flows, WHaT I focus on GROWS.

I WiLL emBRaCe THiS New THOUGHT, BeLief, OR HaBiT

I aSK my HeaRT aND THe UNiVeRSe TO GUiDe me.
TODaY, I am manifeSTiNG THiS (OR SOmeTHiNG BeTTeR)

NOW, I WiLL USe THe POWeR of my imaGiNaTioN TO ViSUaLize iT
COmiNG TRUe. FOR THRee minUTeS, WiTH eyeS CLOSeD, I'LL
exPeRieNCe HOW iT miGHT LOOK, feeL, SmeLL, TaSTe, aND SOUND
aS if iT iS HaPPeNiNG TODaY. I WiLL HaVe fUN DayDReamiNG
fReeLy aND WON'T GeT aTTaCHeD TO SPeCific OUTCOmeS.

NOTeS fROm my ViSUaLizaTioN

TO KeeP my DReam aLiVe, I WiLL focUS ON THiS WORD
OR affiRmaTioN TODaY

ONe iNSPiReD aCTioN I WiLL TaKe iN THe DiReCTioN of my DReam iS

NOW, I SURReNDer aND TRUST. aND SO iT iS.

DAILY 👁 FOCUS

Date _____

Take THREE DEEP BREATHS.

IN THIS moment, I am GRATEFUL FOR

MiRaCLeS aND BLeSSiNGS I am CeLeBRaTiNG (eveN ONeS ON THe way)

I am PROUD of myseLf FOR

ONe THiNG I appReCiaTe aBOUT my BODy is

I aCKNOWLeDGe THeSe emOTiONS I'm feeLiNG RiGHT NOW

ONe THOUGHT, LimiTiNG BeLief, OR HaBiT I WiLL LeT GO of is

WHERE MY ATTENTION GOES, ENERGY flows, WHAT I focus on GROWS.

I WILL EMBRACE THIS NEW THOUGHT, BELIEF, OR HABIT

I ASK MY HEART AND THE UNIVERSE TO GUIDE ME.
TODAY, I AM MANIFESTING THIS (OR SOMETHING BETTER)

NOW, I WILL USE THE POWER OF MY IMAGINATION TO VISUALIZE IT
COMING TRUE. FOR THREE MINUTES, WITH EYES CLOSED, I'LL
EXPERIENCE HOW IT MIGHT LOOK, FEEL, SMELL, TASTE, AND SOUND
AS IF IT IS HAPPENING TODAY. I WILL HAVE FUN DAYDREAMING
FREELY AND WON'T GET ATTACHED TO SPECIFIC OUTCOMES.

NOTES FROM MY VISUALIZATION

TO KEEP MY DREAM ALIVE, I WILL FOCUS ON THIS WORD
OR AFFIRMATION TODAY

ONE INSPIRED ACTION I WILL TAKE IN THE DIRECTION OF MY DREAM IS

NOW, I SURRENDER AND TRUST. AND SO IT IS.

DAILY 👁 FOCUS

Date _____

Take THRee Deep BReaTHS.

In THiS moment, I am GRaTeFuL foR

MiRacLeS aND BLeSSiNGS I am CeLeBRaTiNG (eVeN oNeS oN THe WaY)

I am PROUD of myseLf foR

oNe THiNG I aPPReCiaTe aBOUT my BODy iS

I acKNOWLeDGe THeSe emoTiONS I'm feeLiNG RiGHT NOW

oNe THOUGHT, LimiTiNG BeLief, oR HaBiT I WiLL LeT Go of iS

WHere my ATTeNTioN Goes, eNeRGY flows, WHAT I focus on GROWS.

I WiLL emBRace THiS NeW THOUGHT, BeLief, OR HaBiT

I asK my HeaRT aND THe UNiVeRSe TO GUiDe me.
TODay, I am manifesTiNG THiS (OR SOmeTHiNG BeTTeR)

NOW, I WiLL USe THe POWeR of my imaGiNaTiON TO ViSUaLize iT
COmiNG TRUe. FOR THRee minUTeS, WiTH eyes CLOSeD, I'LL
exPeRieNCe HOW iT miGHT LOOK, feeL, SmeLL, TaSTe, aND SOUND
as if iT iS HaPPeNiNG TODay. I WiLL HaVe fUN DayDReamiNG
fReeLy aND WON'T GeT aTTacHeD TO SPeCific OUTCOmes.

NOTeS fROm my ViSUaLizaTiON

TO KeeP my DReam aLiVe, I WiLL focUS ON THiS WORD
OR affiRmaTiON TODay

ONe iNSPiReD acTiON I WiLL TaKe iN THe DiReCTiON of my DReam iS

NOW, I SURReNDer and TRUST. AND SO iT iS.

DAILY 👁 FOCUS

Date _____

TAKE THREE DEEP BREATHS.

IN THIS moment, I am GRATEFUL FOR

MIRACLES AND BLESSINGS I am CELEBRATING (EVEN ONES ON THE WAY)

I am PROUD OF myself FOR

ONE THING I APPRECIATE ABOUT my BODY IS

I ACKNOWLEDGE THESE emotions I'm feeling RIGHT NOW

ONE THOUGHT, LIMITING BELIEF, OR HABIT I WILL LET GO OF IS

WHere my ATTeNTiON GOeS, eNeRGY flows, WHaT I focus on GROWS.

I WiLL emBRace THiS New THOUGHT, BeLief, OR HaBiT

I asK my HeaRT aND THe UNiveRSe TO GUiDe me.
TODay, I am manifeSTiNG THiS (OR SOmeTHiNG BeTTeR)

Now, I WiLL USe THe POWeR of my imaGiNaTiON TO visuaLize iT
comiNG TRUe. FOR THRee minuTeS, WiTH eyeS cLOSeD, I'LL
eXPeRieNce HOW iT miGHT LOOK, feeL, SmeLL, TaSTe, aND SOUND
as if iT iS HaPPeNiNG TODay. I WiLL Have fUN DayDReamiNG
fReeLy aND WON'T GeT aTTacHeD TO SPecific OUTcomeS.

NOTeS fROm my visuaLizaTiON

TO KeeP my DReam aLive, I WiLL focus ON THiS WORD
OR affirmaTiON TODay

ONe iNSPiReD acTiON I WiLL TaKe iN THe DiRecTiON of my DReam iS

Now, I SURReNDeR aND TRUST. aND SO iT iS.

DAILY 👁 FOCUS

Date _____

Take THReE DeeP BReaTHS.

IN THiS moment, I am GRaTeFuL foR

MiRacLeS aND BLeSSiNGS I am CeLeBRaTiNG (eveN oNeS oN THe way)

I am PROUD of myseLf foR

ONe THiNG I aPPReCiaTe aBOUT my BODy is

I acKNowLeDGe THeSe emoTioNS I'm feeLiNG RiGHT Now

ONe THOUGHT, LimiTiNG BeLief, oR HaBiT I wiLL LeT Go of is

WHeRe MY ATTeNTiON Goes, eNeRGY flows, WHaT I focus on GROWS.

I WILL eMBRaCe THiS NeW THOUGHT, BeLief, OR HaBiT

I aSK my HeaRT aND THe UNiVeRSe TO GUiDe me.
TODay, I am manifeSTiNG THiS (OR SOmeTHiNG BeTTeR)

NOW, I WILL USe THe POWeR of my imaGiNaTiON TO ViSUaLiZe iT
COmiNG TRUe. FOR THRee miNUTeS, WITH eyes CLOSeD, I'LL
eXPeRieNCe HOW iT miGHT LOOK, feeL, SmeLL, TaSTe, aND SOUND
aS if iT iS HaPPeNiNG TODay. I WiLL HaVe fUN DayDReamiNG
fReeLy aND WON'T GeT aTTaCHeD TO SPeCifiC OUTCOmeS.

NOTeS fROm my ViSUaLiZaTiON

TO Keep my DReam aLiVe, I WiLL focUS ON THiS WORD
OR affiRmaTiON TODay

ONe iNSPiReD aCTiON I WiLL TaKe iN THe DiReCTiON of my DReam iS

NOW, I SURReNDeʐ and TRUST. AND SO iT iS.

DAiLY 👁 FOCUS

Date _____

Take THRee Deep BReaths.

In this moment, I am GRateful for

Miracles and Blessings I am celeBRating (even ones on the way)

I am pROUD of myself for

One thing I appReciate about my BODy is

I acKNOWLeDGe these emotions I'm feeling RIGHT NOW

One THOUGHT, Limiting Belief, OR HaBit I will Let GO of is

WHere MY ATTeNTioN GOes, eNeRGY flows, WHAT I focus on GROWS.

I WiLL eMBRace THiS NeW THOUGHT, BeLieƒ, OR HaBiT

I aSK MY HeaRT aND THe UNiVeRSe TO GUiDe Me.
TODay, I aM MANifeSTiNG THiS (OR SOMeTHiNG BeTTeR)

NOW, I WiLL USe THe POWeR of MY iMaGiNaTiON TO ViSUaLiZe iT
coMiNG TRUe. FOR THRee MiNUTeS, WiTH eyeS CLOSeD, I'LL
exPeRieNce HOW iT MiGHT LOOK, feeL, SMeLL, TaSTe, aND SOUND
aS iF iT iS HaPPeNiNG TODay. I WiLL HaVe ƒUN DayDReaMiNG
ƒReeLy aND WON'T GeT aTTaCHeD TO SPeciƒic OUTcOMeS.

NOTeS ƒROM MY ViSUaLiZaTiON

TO KeeP MY DReaM aLiVe, I WiLL ƒOcUS ON THiS WORD
OR aƒƒiRMaTiON TODay

ONe iNSPiReD acTiON I WiLL TaKe iN THe DiRecTiON of MY DReaM iS

NOW, I SURReNDer aND TRUST. AND SO iT iS.

DAILY 👁 FOCUS

Date _____

Take THReE DeeP BReaTHS.

IN THiS moment, I am GRaTefUL foR

MiRacLeS aND BLeSSiNGS I am CeLeBRaTiNG (eveN oNeS oN THe Way)

I am PROUD of myseLf foR

oNe THiNG I appReciaTe aBoUT my BoDy iS

I acKNoWLeDGe THeSe emoTioNS I'm feeLiNG RiGHT NoW

oNe THOUGHT, LimiTiNG BeLief, oR HaBiT I WiLL LeT Go of iS

WHERE MY ATTENTION GOES, ENERGY flows, WHAT I focus on GROWS.

I WILL EMBRACE THIS NEW THOUGHT, BELIEF, OR HABIT

I ASK my HEART AND THE UNIVERSE TO GUIDE me.
TODAY, I AM manifesting THIS (OR something BETTER)

NOW, I WILL USE THE POWER of my IMAGINATION TO VISUALIZE IT
COMING TRUE. FOR THREE minutes, WITH eyes CLOSED, I'LL
EXPERIENCE HOW IT MIGHT LOOK, feel, smell, TASTE, AND SOUND
AS IF IT IS HAPPENING TODAY. I WILL HAVE fUN DayDREAMING
FREELY AND WON'T GET ATTACHED TO SPECIFIC outcomes.

NOTES fROM my VISUALIZATION

TO KEEP my DREAM ALIVE, I WILL focus ON THIS WORD
OR affirmation TODAY

ONE INSPIRED ACTION I WILL TAKE IN THE DIRECTION of my DREAM IS

NOW, I SURRENDER and TRUST. AND SO IT IS.

DAILY 👁 FOCUS

Date _____

Take THREE Deep Breaths.

In this moment, I am grateful for

Miracles and blessings I am celebrating (even ones on the way)

I am proud of myself for

One thing I appreciate about my body is

I acknowledge these emotions I'm feeling right now

One thought, limiting belief, or habit I will let go of is

WHERE MY ATTENTION GOES, ENERGY flows, WHAT I focus on GROWS.

I WILL EMBRACE THIS NEW THOUGHT, BELIEF, OR HABIT

I ASK my HEART AND THE UNIVERSE TO GUIDE me.
TODAY, I AM MANIFESTING THIS (OR SOMETHING BETTER)

NOW, I WILL USE THE POWER OF my IMAGINATION TO VISUALIZE IT
COMING TRUE. FOR THREE MINUTES, WITH eyes CLOSED, I'LL
EXPERIENCE HOW IT MIGHT LOOK, feel, SMELL, TASTE, AND SOUND
AS IF IT IS HAPPENING TODAY. I WILL HAVE fUN DAYDREAMING
fREELY AND WON'T GET ATTACHED TO SPECIFIC OUTCOMES.

NOTES fROM my VISUALIZATION

TO KEEP my DREAM ALIVE, I WILL fOCUS ON THIS WORD
OR affIRMATION TODAY

ONE INSPIRED ACTION I WILL TAKE IN THE DIRECTION of my DREAM IS

NOW, I SURRENDER and TRUST. AND SO IT IS.

DAILY 👁 FOCUS

Date _____

Take THREE DEEP BREATHS.

IN THIS moment, I am GRATEFUL FOR

MIRACLES AND BLESSINGS I am CELEBRATING (EVEN ONES ON THE WAY)

I am PROUD OF myself FOR

ONE THING I appreciate ABOUT my BODY is

I acKNOWLEDGE THESE emotions I'm feeling RIGHT NOW

ONE THOUGHT, LimiTING BELIEF, OR HABIT I WILL LET GO OF is

WHere mY ATTeNTioN Goes, eNeRGY flows, WHAT I focus on GROWS.

I WiLL emBRace THiS NeW THOUGHT, BeLief, OR HaBiT

I asK my HeaRT aND THe UNiVeRSe TO GUide me.
TODay, I am manifeSTING THiS (OR SOmeTHiNG BeTTeR)

NOW, I WiLL USe THe POWeR of my imaGiNaTiON TO viSUaLiZe iT
COmiNG TRUe. FOR THRee miNUTeS, WiTH eyes CLOSeD, I'LL
exPeRieNCe HOW iT miGHT LOOK, feel, Smell, TaSTe, aND SOUND
as if iT iS HaPPeNiNG TODay. I WiLL HaVe fUN DayDReamiNG
fReeLy aND WON'T GeT aTTaCHeD TO SPeCific OUTCOmeS.

NOTeS fROm my viSUaLiZaTiON

TO KeeP my DReam aLive, I WiLL focUS ON THiS WORD
OR affiRmaTiON TODay

ONe iNSPiReD aCTiON I WiLL TaKe iN THe DiReCTiON of my DReam iS

NOW, I SURReNDer aND TRUST. AND SO iT iS.

DAiLY 👁 FOCUS

Date _____

Take THRee DeeP BReaTHS.

IN THiS moment, I am GRaTefUL foR

MiRacLeS aND BLeSSiNGS I am CeLeBRaTiNG (eveN oNeS oN THe way)

I am PROUD of myseLf foR

oNe THiNG I appReciaTe aBOUT my BODY iS

I ackNOwLeDGe THeSe emoTioNS I'm feeLiNG RiGHT Now

oNe THOUGHT, LimiTiNG BeLief, oR HaBiT I wiLL LeT Go of iS

WHERE MY ATTENTION GOES, ENERGY flows, WHAT I focus on GROWS.

I WILL EMBRACE THIS NEW THOUGHT, BELIEF, OR HABIT

I ASK MY HEART AND THE UNIVERSE TO GUIDE ME.
TODAY, I AM MANIFESTING THIS (OR SOMETHING BETTER)

NOW, I WILL USE THE POWER OF MY IMAGINATION TO VISUALIZE IT
COMING TRUE. FOR THREE MINUTES, WITH EYES CLOSED, I'LL
EXPERIENCE HOW IT MIGHT LOOK, FEEL, SMELL, TASTE, AND SOUND
AS IF IT IS HAPPENING TODAY. I WILL HAVE FUN DAYDREAMING
FREELY AND WON'T GET ATTACHED TO SPECIFIC OUTCOMES.

NOTES FROM MY VISUALIZATION

TO KEEP MY DREAM ALIVE, I WILL FOCUS ON THIS WORD
OR AFFIRMATION TODAY

ONE INSPIRED ACTION I WILL TAKE IN THE DIRECTION OF MY DREAM IS

NOW, I SURRENDER and TRUST. AND SO IT IS.

DAILY 👁 FOCUS

Date _____

Take THREE DeeP BReaTHs.

IN THis moment, I am GRaTeFuL foR

MiRacLes aND BLessiNGs I am CeLeBRaTiNG (eveN oNes oN THe way)

I am PROUD of myself foR

oNe THiNG I appReciaTe aBouT my BoDy is

I acKNowLeDGe THese emoTioNs I'm feeLiNG RiGHT Now

oNe THouGHT, LimiTiNG BeLief, oR HaBiT I wiLL LeT Go of is

WHERE MY ATTENTION GOES, ENERGY flows, WHAT I focus on GROWS.

I WILL EMBRACE THIS NEW THOUGHT, BELIEF, OR HABIT

I ASK MY HEART AND THE UNIVERSE TO GUIDE ME.
TODAY, I AM MANIFESTING THIS (OR SOMETHING BETTER)

NOW, I WILL USE THE POWER OF MY IMAGINATION TO VISUALIZE IT COMING TRUE. FOR THREE MINUTES, WITH EYES CLOSED, I'LL EXPERIENCE HOW IT MIGHT LOOK, FEEL, SMELL, TASTE, AND SOUND AS IF IT IS HAPPENING TODAY. I WILL HAVE FUN DAYDREAMING FREELY AND WON'T GET ATTACHED TO SPECIFIC OUTCOMES.

NOTES FROM MY VISUALIZATION

TO KEEP MY DREAM ALIVE, I WILL FOCUS ON THIS WORD
OR AFFIRMATION TODAY

ONE INSPIRED ACTION I WILL TAKE IN THE DIRECTION OF MY DREAM IS

NOW, I SURRENDER and TRUST. AND SO IT IS.

DAiLY 👁 FOCUS

Date _____

Take THReE Deep BReaTHS.

In THiS moment, I am GRaTefuL foR

MiRacLeS and BLeSSinGS I am ceLeBRaTinG (even oneS on THe way)

I am PROUD of myseLf foR

one THinG I appReciaTe aBouT my BoDy iS

I acKnowLeDGe THeSe emoTionS I'm feeLinG RiGHT now

one THouGHT, LimiTinG BeLief, oR HaBiT I wiLL LeT Go of iS

WHERE MY ATTENTION GOES, ENERGY flows, WHAT I focus on GROWS.

I WILL EMBRACE THIS NEW THOUGHT, BELIEF, OR HABIT

I ASK MY HEART AND THE UNIVERSE TO GUIDE ME.
TODAY, I AM MANIFESTING THIS (OR SOMETHING BETTER)

NOW, I WILL USE THE POWER OF MY IMAGINATION TO VISUALIZE IT COMING TRUE. FOR THREE MINUTES, WITH EYES CLOSED, I'LL EXPERIENCE HOW IT MIGHT LOOK, FEEL, SMELL, TASTE, AND SOUND AS IF IT IS HAPPENING TODAY. I WILL HAVE FUN DAYDREAMING FREELY AND WON'T GET ATTACHED TO SPECIFIC OUTCOMES.

NOTES FROM MY VISUALIZATION

TO KEEP MY DREAM ALIVE, I WILL FOCUS ON THIS WORD OR AFFIRMATION TODAY

ONE INSPIRED ACTION I WILL TAKE IN THE DIRECTION OF MY DREAM IS

NOW, I SURRENDER and TRUST. AND SO IT IS.

DAILY 👁 FOCUS

Date _____

Take THREE DeeP BReaTHS.

IN THiS moment, I am GRaTeful foR

MiRacLes and BLeSSINGS I am CeLeBRaTing (even ones ON THe way)

I am PROUD of myseLf foR

One THiNG I aPPReCiaTe aBOUT my BODy iS

I acKNOWLeDGe THeSe emOTiONS I'm feeLiNG RiGHT NOW

One THOUGHT, LimiTiNG BeLief, OR HaBiT I WiLL LeT GO of iS

WHERE MY ATTENTION GOES, ENERGY flows, WHAT I focus on GROWS.

I WILL EMBRACE THIS NEW THOUGHT, BELIEF, OR HABIT

I ASK MY HEART AND THE UNIVERSE TO GUIDE ME.
TODAY, I AM MANIFESTING THIS (OR SOMETHING BETTER)

NOW, I WILL USE THE POWER OF MY IMAGINATION TO VISUALIZE IT
COMING TRUE. FOR THREE MINUTES, WITH EYES CLOSED, I'LL
EXPERIENCE HOW IT MIGHT LOOK, FEEL, SMELL, TASTE, AND SOUND
AS IF IT IS HAPPENING TODAY. I WILL HAVE FUN DAYDREAMING
FREELY AND WON'T GET ATTACHED TO SPECIFIC OUTCOMES.

NOTES FROM MY VISUALIZATION

TO KEEP MY DREAM ALIVE, I WILL FOCUS ON THIS WORD
OR AFFIRMATION TODAY

ONE INSPIRED ACTION I WILL TAKE IN THE DIRECTION OF MY DREAM IS

NOW, I SURRENDER and TRUST. AND SO IT IS.

DAiLY 👁 FOCUS

Date _____

Take THRee DeeP BReaTHs.

In THis moment, I am GRaTefuL foR

MiRacLes anD BLessinGs I am CeLeBRaTinG (even ones on THe way)

I am PROUD of myseLf foR

one THinG I appReciaTe aBoUT my BoDy is

I acknowLeDGe THese emoTions I'm feeLinG RiGHT now

one THOUGHT, LimiTinG BeLief, oR HaBiT I wiLL LeT Go of is

WHERE MY ATTENTION GOES, ENERGY flows, WHAT I focus on GROWS.

I WILL EMBRACE THIS NEW THOUGHT, BELIEF, OR HABIT

I ask MY HEART AND THE UNIVERSE TO GUIDE ME.
TODAY, I am manifesting THIS (OR SOMETHING BETTER)

NOW, I WILL USE THE POWER OF MY imagination TO visualize IT
COMING TRUE. FOR THREE MINUTES, WITH eyes CLOSED, I'LL
EXPERIENCE HOW IT MIGHT LOOK, feel, SMELL, TASTE, AND SOUND
as if IT IS HAPPENING TODAY. I WILL HAVE fUN DaYDREaming
fREELy AND WON'T GET ATTACHED TO SPECIFIC OUTCOMES.

NOTES fROM MY VISUALIZATION

TO KEEP MY DREAM aLive, I WILL fOCUS ON THIS WORD
OR affIRMATION TODAY

ONE INSPIRED ACTION I WILL TAKE IN THE DIRECTION Of MY DREAM is

NOW, I SURRENDER and TRUST. AND SO iT iS.

DAILY 👁 FOCUS

Date _____

Take THREE Deep BREaTHS.

IN THIS moment, I am GRaTeful foR

MiRacLes aND BLeSSiNGS I am CeLeBRaTiNG (eveN oNeS oN THe way)

I am PROUD of myself foR

oNe THING I aPPReCiaTe aBOUT my BODy iS

I acKNowLeDGe THeSe emoTioNS I'm feeLiNG RiGHT Now

oNe THOUGHT, LimiTiNG BeLief, oR HaBiT I WiLL LeT Go of iS

WHERE MY ATTENTION GOES, ENERGY flows, WHAT I focus on GROWS.

I WILL EMBRACE THIS NEW THOUGHT, BELIEF, OR HABIT

I ASK MY HEART AND THE UNIVERSE TO GUIDE ME.
TODAY, I AM MANIFESTING THIS (OR SOMETHING BETTER)

NOW, I WILL USE THE POWER OF MY IMAGINATION TO VISUALIZE IT
COMING TRUE. FOR THREE MINUTES, WITH EYES CLOSED, I'LL
EXPERIENCE HOW IT MIGHT LOOK, FEEL, SMELL, TASTE, AND SOUND
AS IF IT IS HAPPENING TODAY. I WILL HAVE FUN DAYDREAMING
FREELY AND WON'T GET ATTACHED TO SPECIFIC OUTCOMES.

NOTES FROM MY VISUALIZATION

TO KEEP MY DREAM ALIVE, I WILL FOCUS ON THIS WORD
OR AFFIRMATION TODAY

ONE INSPIRED ACTION I WILL TAKE IN THE DIRECTION OF MY DREAM IS

NOW, I SURRENDER and TRUST. AND SO IT IS.

DAILY 👁 FOCUS

Date _____

Take THREE DEEP BREaTHS.

IN THiS moment, I am GRaTeFUL FOR

Miracles and BLESSINGS I am CELEBRATING (even ONES ON THE way)

I am PROUD of myself FOR

ONE THING I appreciate aBOUT my BODY is

I acKNOWLEDGE THESE emOTIONS I'm feeliNG RIGHT NOW

ONE THOUGHT, LimiTiNG BELief, OR HaBiT I WiLL LET GO of is

WHERE MY ATTENTION GOES, ENERGY FLOWS, WHAT I FOCUS ON GROWS.

I WILL EMBRACE THIS NEW THOUGHT, BELIEF, OR HABIT

I ASK MY HEART AND THE UNIVERSE TO GUIDE ME.
TODAY, I AM MANIFESTING THIS (OR SOMETHING BETTER)

NOW, I WILL USE THE POWER OF MY IMAGINATION TO VISUALIZE IT
COMING TRUE. FOR THREE MINUTES, WITH EYES CLOSED, I'LL
EXPERIENCE HOW IT MIGHT LOOK, FEEL, SMELL, TASTE, AND SOUND
AS IF IT IS HAPPENING TODAY. I WILL HAVE FUN DAYDREAMING
FREELY AND WON'T GET ATTACHED TO SPECIFIC OUTCOMES.

NOTES FROM MY VISUALIZATION

TO KEEP MY DREAM ALIVE, I WILL FOCUS ON THIS WORD
OR AFFIRMATION TODAY

ONE INSPIRED ACTION I WILL TAKE IN THE DIRECTION OF MY DREAM IS

NOW, I SURRENDER and TRUST. AND SO IT IS.

DAiLY 👁 FOCUS

Date _____

Take THRee DeeP BReaTHs.

In THis moment, I am GRaTeFuL foR

Miracles and BLessinGs I am CeLeBRaTinG (even ones on THe way)

I am PROUD of myseLf foR

One THinG I appReCiaTe aBouT my BODy is

I aCKNOWLeDGe THese emOTions I'm feeLinG RiGHT Now

One THOUGHT, LimiTinG BeLief, OR HaBiT I WiLL LeT Go of is

WHERE MY ATTENTION GOES, ENERGY flows, WHAT I focus on GROWS.

I WILL EMBRACE THIS NEW THOUGHT, BELIEF, OR HABIT

I ASK MY HEART AND THE UNIVERSE TO GUIDE ME.
TODAY, I AM MANIFESTING THIS (OR SOMETHING BETTER)

NOW, I WILL USE THE POWER OF MY IMAGINATION TO VISUALIZE IT
COMING TRUE. FOR THREE MINUTES, WITH EYES CLOSED, I'LL
EXPERIENCE HOW IT MIGHT LOOK, FEEL, SMELL, TASTE, AND SOUND
AS IF IT IS HAPPENING TODAY. I WILL HAVE FUN DAYDREAMING
FREELY AND WON'T GET ATTACHED TO SPECIFIC OUTCOMES.

NOTES FROM MY VISUALIZATION

TO KEEP MY DREAM ALIVE, I WILL FOCUS ON THIS WORD
OR AFFIRMATION TODAY

ONE INSPIRED ACTION I WILL TAKE IN THE DIRECTION OF MY DREAM IS

NOW, I SURRENDER and TRUST. AND SO IT IS.

DAiLY 👁 FOCUS

Date _____

Take THREE Deep BReaTHs.

In THis moment, I am GRaTeful foR

Miracles and Blessings I am celebrating (even ones on the way)

I am PROUD of myself foR

One THinG I appreciate aBout my BODy is

I acknowledge THese emotions I'm feeling RIGHT Now

One THOUGHT, limiting Belief, OR HaBiT I Will Let Go of is

WHere mY ATTeNTioN Goes, eNerGY flows, WHAT I focus on GROWS.

I WiLL emBRace THiS NeW THOUGHT, BeLief, OR HaBiT

I aSK my HeaRT AND THe UNiVeRSe TO GUiDe me.
TODay, I am manifeSTiNG THiS (OR SOMeTHiNG BeTTeR)

NOW, I WiLL USe THe POWeR of my imaGiNATiON TO ViSUaLize iT
COmiNG TRUe. FOR THRee minUTeS, WiTH eyeS CLOSeD, I'LL
exPeRieNCe HOW iT miGHT LOOK, feeL, SmeLL, TaSTe, AND SOUND
aS if iT iS HaPPeNiNG TODay. I WiLL HaVe fUN DayDReamiNG
fReeLy AND WON'T GeT aTTacHeD TO SPeCific OUTCOmeS.

NOTeS fROm my ViSUaLizaTiON

TO KeeP my DReam aLiVe, I WiLL fOCUS ON THiS WORD
OR affiRmaTiON TODay

ONe iNSPiReD acTiON I WiLL TaKe iN THe DiReCTiON of my DReam iS

NOW, I SURReNDer and TRUST. AND SO iT iS.

DAILY 👁 FOCUS

Date _____

Take THREE DEEP BREATHS.

IN THIS moment, I am GRATEFUL FOR

MiRACLES AND BLESSINGS I am CELEBRATING (even ONES ON THE way)

I am PROUD Of myself FOR

ONE THING I appreciate aBOUT my BODY is

I ACKNOWLEDGE THESE emoTIONS I'm feeling RIGHT NOW

ONE THOUGHT, LimiTING Belief, OR HaBiT I WILL LET GO Of is

WHERE MY ATTENTION GOES, ENERGY flows, WHAT I focus on GROWS.

I WILL EMBRACE THIS NEW THOUGHT, BELIEF, OR HABIT

I ASK MY HEART AND THE UNIVERSE TO GUIDE ME.
TODAY, I AM MANIFESTING THIS (OR SOMETHING BETTER)

NOW, I WILL USE THE POWER OF MY IMAGINATION TO VISUALIZE IT
COMING TRUE. FOR THREE MINUTES, WITH EYES CLOSED, I'LL
EXPERIENCE HOW IT MIGHT LOOK, FEEL, SMELL, TASTE, AND SOUND
AS IF IT IS HAPPENING TODAY. I WILL HAVE FUN DAYDREAMING
FREELY AND WON'T GET ATTACHED TO SPECIFIC OUTCOMES.

NOTES FROM MY VISUALIZATION

TO KEEP MY DREAM ALIVE, I WILL FOCUS ON THIS WORD
OR AFFIRMATION TODAY

ONE INSPIRED ACTION I WILL TAKE IN THE DIRECTION OF MY DREAM IS

NOW, I SURRENDER AND TRUST. AND SO IT IS.

DAiLY 👁 FOCUS

Date _____

Take THRee Deep BReaTHs.

In THis moment, I am GRaTefuL foR

MiRacLes and BLessinGs I am CeLeBRaTinG (even ones on THe way)

I am PROUD of myseLf foR

One THinG I appReciaTe aBOUT my BODy is

I acknowLeDGe THese emoTions I'm feeLinG RiGHT now

One THOUGHT, LimiTinG BeLief, OR HaBiT I wiLL LeT GO of is

WHere my ATTeNTiON GOes, eNERGY flows, WHaT I focus oN GROWS.

I WiLL emBRaCe THiS NeW THOUGHT, BeLief, OR HaBiT

I aSK my HeaRT aND THe UNiVeRSe TO GUiDe me.
TODay, I am maNifeSTiNG THiS (OR SOmeTHiNG BeTTeR)

NOW, I WiLL USe THe POWeR of my imaGiNaTiON TO ViSUaLiZe iT
COmiNG TRUe. FOR THRee miNUTeS, WiTH eyeS CLOSeD, I'LL
exPeRieNCe HOW iT miGHT LOOK, feel, SmeLL, TaSTe, aND SOUND
aS if iT iS HaPPeNiNG TODay. I WiLL HaVe fUN DayDReamiNG
fReeLy aND WON'T GeT aTTaCHeD TO SPeCifiC OUTCOmeS.

NOTeS fROm my ViSUaLiZaTiON

TO Keep my DReam aLiVe, I WiLL focUS ON THiS WORD
OR affiRmaTiON TODay

ONe iNSPiReD aCTiON I WiLL TaKe iN THe DiReCTiON of my DReam iS

NOW, I SURReNDeR aND TRUST. aND SO iT iS.

DAILY 👁 FOCUS

Date _____

Take THREE Deep Breaths.

In this moment, I am grateful for

Miracles and blessings I am celebrating (even ones on the way)

I am proud of myself for

One thing I appreciate about my body is

I acknowledge these emotions I'm feeling right now

One thought, limiting belief, or habit I will let go of is

WHERE MY ATTENTION GOES, ENERGY flows, WHAT I focus on GROWS.

I WILL EMBRACE THIS NEW THOUGHT, BELIEF, OR HABIT

I ASK my HEART AND THE UNIVERSE TO GUIDE me.
TODAY, I AM MANIFESTING THIS (OR SOMETHING BETTER)

NOW, I WILL USE THE POWER OF my IMAGINATION TO VISUALIZE IT
COMING TRUE. FOR THREE MINUTES, WITH eyes CLOSED, I'LL
EXPERIENCE HOW IT MIGHT LOOK, feel, SMELL, TASTE, AND SOUND
AS IF IT IS HAPPENING TODAY. I WILL HAVE fUN DAYDREAMING
fREELY AND WON'T GET ATTACHED TO SPECIFIC OUTCOMES.

NOTES fROM my VISUALIZATION

TO KEEP my DREAM ALIVE, I WILL fOCUS ON THIS WORD
OR AffIRMATION TODAY

ONE INSPIRED ACTION I WILL TAKE IN THE DIRECTION OF my DREAM IS

NOW, I SURRENDER and TRUST. AND SO IT IS.

DAILY 👁 FOCUS

Date _____

Take THREE Deep BReaTHs.

In THis moment, I am GRaTeful foR

MiRacLes and BLessinGs I am CeLeBRaTinG (even ones on THe way)

I am pRoud of myself foR

One THinG I appReciaTe aBouT my Body is

I acKnowLedGe THese emotions I'm feeLinG RiGHT now

One THOUGHT, LimiTinG BeLief, OR HaBiT I wiLL LeT GO of is

WHERE MY ATTENTION GOES, ENERGY flows, WHAT I focus on GROWS.

I WILL EMBRACE THIS NEW THOUGHT, BELIEF, OR HABIT

I ASK my HEART AND THE UNIVERSE TO GUIDE me.
TODAY, I AM manifesting THIS (OR SOMETHING BETTER)

NOW, I WILL USE THE POWER of my imaGination TO visualize iT
COMING TRUE. FOR THREE minutes, WITH eyes CLOSED, I'LL
experience HOW iT miGHT LOOK, feel, smell, TASTe, AND SOUND
as if iT is HaPPeNiNG ToDay. I WILL Have fUN DayDREAMING
fReeLy AND WON'T GeT aTTacHeD TO SPeCific ouTcomes.

NOTES fROm my VISUALIZATION

TO keep my DREAM aLive, I WILL focus on THIS WORD
OR affirmation TODAY

ONe iNSPiReD acTioN I WILL TaKe iN THE DiRecTion of my DReam is

NOW, I SURReNDer and TRUST. AND so iT iS.

DAILY 👁 FOCUS

Date _____

Take THREE DEEP BREATHS.

In THIS moment, I am GRATEFUL FOR

MiRACLES AND BLESSINGS I am CELEBRATING (EVEN ONES ON THE WAY)

I am PROUD of myself FOR

ONE THING I aPPRECIATE ABOUT my BODY is

I aCKNOWLEDGE THESE emOTIONS I'm FEELING RIGHT NOW

ONE THOUGHT, LIMITING BELIEF, OR HABIT I WILL LET GO of is

WHERE MY ATTENTION GOES, ENERGY flows, WHAT I focus on GROWS.

I WILL EMBRACE THIS NEW THOUGHT, BELIEF, OR HABIT

I ASK MY HEART AND THE UNIVERSE TO GUIDE ME.
TODAY, I AM MANIFESTING THIS (OR SOMETHING BETTER)

NOW, I WILL USE THE POWER OF MY IMAGINATION TO VISUALIZE IT
COMING TRUE. FOR THREE MINUTES, WITH EYES CLOSED, I'LL
EXPERIENCE HOW IT MIGHT LOOK, FEEL, SMELL, TASTE, AND SOUND
AS IF IT IS HAPPENING TODAY. I WILL HAVE FUN DAYDREAMING
FREELY AND WON'T GET ATTACHED TO SPECIFIC OUTCOMES.

NOTES FROM MY VISUALIZATION

TO KEEP MY DREAM ALIVE, I WILL FOCUS ON THIS WORD
OR AFFIRMATION TODAY

ONE INSPIRED ACTION I WILL TAKE IN THE DIRECTION OF MY DREAM IS

NOW, I SURRENDER and TRUST. AND SO IT IS.

DAiLY 👁 FOCUS

Date _____

Take THRee Deep BReaTHs.

In THis moment, I am GRaTeful foR

MiRacLes and BLessinGs I am CeleBRaTinG (even ones on THe way)

I am PROUD of myself foR

One THinG I appReciaTe aBOUT my BODy is

I acknowLedGe THese emoTions I'm feelinG RiGHT now

One THOUGHT, LimiTinG Belief, OR HaBiT I wiLL LeT Go of is

WHere MY ATTeNTioN Goes, eNeRGY flows, WHAT I focus on GROWS.

I WiLL eMBRace THiS New THOUGHT, BeLief, OR HaBiT

I aSK my HeaRT aND THe UNiveRSe To GUiDe me.
ToDay, I am maNifeSTiNG THiS (OR SOmeTHiNG BeTTeR)

Now, I WiLL USe THe PoweR of my imaGiNaTioN To viSUaLiZe iT
comiNG TRUe. FOR THRee miNUTeS, WiTH eyes CLOSeD, I'LL
eXPeRieNCe How iT miGHT LooK, feeL, SmeLL, TaSTe, aND SOUND
aS if iT iS HaPPeNiNG ToDay. I WiLL Have fUN DayDReamiNG
fReeLy aND WON'T GeT aTTaCHeD To SPeCific oUTComes.

NoTeS fROm my viSUaLiZaTioN

To KeeP my DReam aLive, I WiLL foCUS ON THiS WORD
OR affiRmaTioN ToDay

ONe iNSPiReD aCTioN I WiLL TaKe iN THe DiReCTioN of my DReam iS

Now, I SURReNDer aND TRUST. AND So iT iS.

DAILY 👁 FOCUS

Date _____

Take THREE DeeP BReaTHS.

IN THiS moment, I am GRaTefuL foR

MiRacLes aND BLeSSiNGS I am CeLeBRaTiNG (eveN oNeS oN THe way)

I am PROUD of myseLf foR

oNe THiNG I appReciaTe aBOUT my BODy is

I ackNowLeDGe THeSe emoTioNS I'm feeLiNG RiGHT NOW

oNe THOUGHT, LimiTiNG BeLief, oR HaBiT I wiLL LeT Go of is

WHERE MY ATTENTION GOES, ENERGY flows, WHAT I focus on GROWS.

I WILL EMBRACE THIS NEW THOUGHT, BELIEF, OR HABIT

I ASK my HEART AND THE UNIVERSE TO GUIDE me.
TODAY, I AM MANIFESTING THIS (OR SOMETHING BETTER)

NOW, I WILL USE THE POWER OF my IMAGINATION TO VISUALIZE IT
COMING TRUE. FOR THREE MINUTES, WITH eyes CLOSED, I'LL
EXPERIENCE HOW IT MIGHT LOOK, FEEL, SMELL, TASTE, AND SOUND
AS IF IT IS HAPPENING TODAY. I WILL HAVE FUN DAYDREAMING
FREELY AND WON'T GET ATTACHED TO SPECIFIC OUTCOMES.

NOTES FROM my VISUALIZATION

TO KEEP my DREAM ALIVE, I WILL FOCUS ON THIS WORD
OR AFFIRMATION TODAY

ONE INSPIRED ACTION I WILL TAKE IN THE DIRECTION OF my DREAM IS

NOW, I SURRENDER and TRUST. AND SO IT IS.

MOON MAGIC

Use these pages to write, draw, or paint about your moon ritual and what you experience.

NEW MOON RITUAL

Date _____

FULL MOON RiTUAL

Date _____

60-DAY CHECK-IN

Reflect

WHAT HAS BEEN THE BIGGEST IMPACT OF THIS PRACTICE FOR ME?

WHAT HAVE I LEARNED ABOUT MYSELF AND MY DESIRES?

WHAT DID MY HEART AND THE UNIVERSE TEACH ME?

CLEAR and ReLeaSe

HAVE I STRUGGLED WITH ANY ASPECT OF THIS PRACTICE? WHY?

AM I BUMPING INTO ANY CONSISTENT, BROADER LIMITING
BELIEFS, DOUBTS, OR FEARS WHILE DREAMING AND VISUALIZING?
WHERE DO THEY COME FROM?

HOW CAN I GIVE MYSELF ADDITIONAL SUPPORT IN HEALING
AND RELEASING LIMITING BELIEFS AND STUCK EMOTIONS?

CELEBRATE

IN THE LAST 30 DAYS, WHAT ARE SOME BEAUTIFUL MOMENTS, BLESSINGS, AND MANIFESTATIONS THAT HAVE OCCURRED?

WHAT ARE SOME MAJOR ASPECTS OF MY LIFE THAT I AM GRATEFUL FOR AND PROUD OF?

WHAT DO I LOVE MOST ABOUT MYSELF? WHAT DO I LOVE MOST ABOUT MY BODY?

CREATE

WHAT ARE MY GREATEST DREAMS AND DESIRES FOR THE NEXT 30 DAYS?

HOW DO I WANT TO FEEL FOR THE NEXT 30 DAYS?

WHAT AM I LOOKING FORWARD TO IN THE NEXT 30 DAYS?

DAILY 👁 FOCUS

Date _____

Take THREE Deep Breaths.

In this moment, I am grateful for

Miracles and Blessings I am celebrating (even ones on the way)

I am proud of myself for

One thing I appreciate about my body is

I acknowledge these emotions I'm feeling right now

One thought, limiting belief, or habit I will let go of is

WHERE MY ATTENTION GOES, ENERGY flows, WHAT I focus on GROWS.

I WILL EMBRACE THIS NEW THOUGHT, BELIEF, OR HABIT

I ASK my HEART AND THE UNIVERSE TO GUIDE ME.
TODAY, I AM MANIFESTING THIS (OR SOMETHING BETTER)

NOW, I WILL USE THE POWER OF my IMAGINATION TO VISUALIZE IT
COMING TRUE. FOR THREE MINUTES, WITH eyes CLOSED, I'LL
EXPERIENCE HOW IT MIGHT LOOK, feel, SMELL, TASTE, AND SOUND
AS IF IT IS HAPPENING TODAY. I WILL HAVE fUN DAYDREAMING
FREELY AND WON'T GET ATTACHED TO SPECIFIC OUTCOMES.

NOTES fROM my VISUALIZATION

TO KEEP my DREAM ALIVE, I WILL fOCUS ON THIS WORD
OR AffIRMATION TODAY

ONE INSPIRED ACTION I WILL TAKE IN THE DIRECTION Of my DREAM IS

NOW, I SURRENDER and TRUST. AND SO IT IS.

DAILY ⊙ FOCUS

Date _____

Take THREE DEEP BREATHS.

In THIS moment, I am GRATEfUL foR

MiRacLeS aND BLeSSiNGS I am CeLeBRaTiNG (even oNes oN THe way)

I am PROUD of myseLf foR

One THiNG I appReciaTe aBOUT my BODY iS

I acKNOWLeDGe THeSe emoTiONS I'm feeLiNG RiGHT NOW

One THOUGHT, LimiTiNG BeLief, oR HaBiT I WiLL LeT GO of iS

WHERE MY ATTENTION GOES, ENERGY flows, WHAT I focus on GROWS.

I WILL EMBRACE THIS NEW THOUGHT, BELIEF, OR HABIT

I ASK MY HEART AND THE UNIVERSE TO GUIDE ME.
TODAY, I AM MANIFESTING THIS (OR SOMETHING BETTER)

NOW, I WILL USE THE POWER OF MY IMAGINATION TO VISUALIZE IT
COMING TRUE. FOR THREE MINUTES, WITH EYES CLOSED, I'LL
EXPERIENCE HOW IT MIGHT LOOK, FEEL, SMELL, TASTE, AND SOUND
AS IF IT IS HAPPENING TODAY. I WILL HAVE FUN DAYDREAMING
FREELY AND WON'T GET ATTACHED TO SPECIFIC OUTCOMES.

NOTES FROM MY VISUALIZATION

TO KEEP MY DREAM ALIVE, I WILL FOCUS ON THIS WORD
OR AFFIRMATION TODAY

ONE INSPIRED ACTION I WILL TAKE IN THE DIRECTION OF MY DREAM IS

NOW, I SURRENDER and TRUST. AND SO IT IS.

DAILY 👁 FOCUS

Date _____

Take THREE DEEP BREATHS.

IN THIS moment, I am GRATEFUL FOR

MiRaCLes aND BLessiNGs I am CeLeBRaTiNG (even ONes ON THe way)

I am PROUD of myself FOR

ONe THiNG I aPPReCiaTe aBOUT my BODy is

I aCKNOWLeDGe THese emoTiONs I'm feeLiNG RiGHT NOW

ONe THOUGHT, LimiTiNG BeLief, OR HaBiT I WiLL LeT GO of is

WHere my ATTENTion Goes, energy flows, WHAT I focus on GROWS.

I WILL emBRace THis new THOUGHT, Belief, or HaBit

I ask my HeaRT aND THe UNiveRse TO GUide me.
TODay, I am manifesTiNG THis (OR somETHING BeTTeR)

NOw, I WILL Use THe POweR of my imaGiNaTion TO visuaLize iT comiNG TRUe. FOR THRee minUTes, WiTH eyes CLOseD, I'LL expeRience HOw iT miGHT LOOK, feeL, smeLL, TasTe, aND SOUND as if iT is HappeNiNG TODay. I WiLL Have fUN DayDReamiNG fReeLy aND WON'T GeT aTTacHeD TO speCific OUTComes.

NOTes fROm my visuaLizaTion

TO Keep my DReam aLive, I WiLL focUs ON THis WORD OR affiRmaTion TODay

ONe iNspiReD acTion I WiLL TaKe iN THe DiRecTion of my DReam is

NOw, I SURReNDer and TRUST. AND so iT is.

DAILY 👁 FOCUS

Date _____

Take THREE Deep BREaTHS.

In THIS moment, I am GRaTefuL foR

MiRacLeS aND BLeSSiNGS I am CeLeBRaTiNG (even ones on THe way)

I am PROUD of myseLf foR

ONe THING I aPPReciaTe aBOUT my BODy iS

I acKNOWLeDGe THeSe emoTiONS I'm feeLiNG RiGHT NOW

ONe THOUGHT, LimiTiNG BeLief, OR HaBiT I WiLL LeT GO of iS

WHERE MY ATTENTION GOES, ENERGY flows, WHAT I focus on GROWS.

I WILL EMBRACE THIS NEW THOUGHT, BELIEF, OR HABIT

I ASK MY HEART AND THE UNIVERSE TO GUIDE ME.
TODAY, I AM MANIFESTING THIS (OR SOMETHING BETTER)

NOW, I WILL USE THE POWER OF MY IMAGINATION TO VISUALIZE IT
COMING TRUE. FOR THREE MINUTES, WITH EYES CLOSED, I'LL
EXPERIENCE HOW IT MIGHT LOOK, FEEL, SMELL, TASTE, AND SOUND
AS IF IT IS HAPPENING TODAY. I WILL HAVE FUN DAYDREAMING
FREELY AND WON'T GET ATTACHED TO SPECIFIC OUTCOMES.

NOTES FROM MY VISUALIZATION

TO KEEP MY DREAM ALIVE, I WILL FOCUS ON THIS WORD
OR AFFIRMATION TODAY

ONE INSPIRED ACTION I WILL TAKE IN THE DIRECTION OF MY DREAM IS

NOW, I SURRENDER and TRUST. AND SO IT IS.

DAILY 👁 FOCUS

Date _____

Take THRee DeeP BReaTHs.

In THis moment, I am GRaTeFuL FoR

MiRacLes anD BLessinGs I am CeLeBRaTinG (even ones on THe way)

I am PRouD oF myseLF FoR

One THinG I appRecIaTe aBouT my BoDy is

I acKnowLeDGe THese emoTions I'm FeeLinG RIGHT now

One THouGHT, LimiTinG BeLieF, oR HaBiT I wiLL LeT Go oF is

WHeRe MY ATTeNTiON GoeS, eNeRGY flows, WHAT I foCuS on GROWS.

I WiLL emBRaCe THiS NeW THOUGHT, BeLieF, OR HaBiT

I aSK my HeaRT AND THe UNiVeRSe To GuiDe me.
TODay, I am manifeSTiNG THiS (OR SOmeTHiNG BeTTeR)

NOW, I WiLL USe THe POWeR of my imaGiNATiON To ViSUaLize iT
COminG TRUe. FOR THRee minUTeS, WiTH eyes CLOSeD, I'LL
exPeRieNCe HOW iT miGHT LOOK, feel, Smell, TaSTe, AND SOUND
aS if iT iS HaPPeNiNG TODay. I WiLL HaVe fUN DayDReaminG
fReeLy AND WON'T GeT aTTaCHeD To SPeCific OUTCOmeS.

NOTeS fROm my ViSUaLizaTiON

TO KeeP my DReam aLiVe, I WiLL foCUS ON THiS WORD
OR affiRmaTiON TODay

ONe iNSPiReD aCTiON I WiLL TaKe iN THe DiReCTiON of my DReam iS

NOW, I SURReNDer and TRUST. AND SO iT iS.

DAiLY 👁 FOCUS

Date _____

Take THReE DeeP BReaTHs.

IN THis moment, I am GRaTefuL foR

MiRacLes aND BLessiNGs I am ceLeBRaTiNG (eveN oNes oN THe way)

I am PROUD of myseLf foR

oNe THiNG I appReciaTe aBouT my BoDy is

I acKNowLeDGe THese emoTioNs I'm feeLiNG RiGHT Now

oNe THOUGHT, LimiTiNG BeLief, oR HaBiT I wiLL LeT Go of is

WHere MY ATTeNTioN Goes, eNeRGY flows, WHAT I focus on GROWS.

I WiLL eMBRaCe THiS NeW THOUGHT, BeLief, OR HaBiT

I aSK MY HeaRT AND THe UNiVeRSe TO GUiDe Me.
TODay, I aM ManifeSTiNG THiS (OR SOMeTHiNG BeTTeR)

NOW, I WiLL USe THe POWeR of MY iMaGiNATiON TO ViSUaLiZe iT
COMiNG TRUe. FOR THRee MiNUTeS, WiTH eyeS CLOSeD, I'LL
eXPeRieNCe HOW iT MiGHT LOOK, feeL, SMeLL, TaSTe, AND SOUND
aS if iT iS HaPPeNiNG TODay. I WiLL HaVe fUN DayDReaMiNG
fReeLy AND WON'T GeT aTTaCHeD TO SPeCific OUTCOMeS.

NOTeS fROM MY ViSUaLiZaTiON

TO KeeP MY DReaM aLiVe, I WiLL focUS ON THiS WORD
OR affiRMaTiON TODay

ONe iNSPiReD aCTiON I WiLL TaKe iN THe DiReCTiON of MY DReaM iS

NOW, I SURReNDeR and TRUST. AND SO iT iS.

DAILY 👁 FOCUS

Date _____

Take THREE DEEP BREATHS.

In THIS moment, I am GRATEFUL for

Miracles and Blessings I am Celebrating (even ones on the way)

I am PROUD of myself for

One THING I appreciate about my BODY is

I acknowledge THESE emotions I'm feeling RIGHT NOW

One THOUGHT, Limiting Belief, OR HABIT I will let GO of is

WHere MY ATTeNTioN Goes, eNeRGY flows, WHaT I focus on GROWS.

I WiLL eMBRaCe THiS NeW THOUGHT, BeLief, OR HaBiT

I aSK MY HeaRT aND THe UNiVeRSe TO GUiDe Me.
TODaY, I aM maNifeSTiNG THiS (OR SOMeTHiNG BeTTeR)

NOW, I WiLL USe THe POWeR of MY imaGiNaTiON TO ViSUaLiZe iT COMiNG TRUe. FOR THRee MiNUTeS, WiTH eyeS CLOSeD, I'LL eXPeRieNCe HOW iT MiGHT LOOK, feeL, SMeLL, TaSTe, aND SOUND aS if iT iS HaPPeNiNG TODaY. I WiLL HaVe fUN DayDReaMiNG fReeLY aND WON'T GeT aTTaCHeD TO SPeCifiC oUTCOMeS.

NOTeS fROM MY ViSUaLiZaTiON

TO KeeP MY DReaM aLiVe, I WiLL foCUS ON THiS WORD OR affiRMaTiON TODaY

ONe iNSPiReD aCTiON I WiLL TaKe iN THe DiReCTiON of MY DReaM iS

NOW, I SURReNDer and TRUST. AND SO iT iS.

DAILY 👁 FOCUS

Date _____

Take THREE Deep BReaTHS.

IN THiS moment, I am GRaTeful foR

MiRacles and BLeSSiNGS I am CeLeBRaTiNG (even ones on THe way)

I am PROUD of myself foR

One THiNG I appRecíaTe aBOUT my BODy is

I acknowLeDGe THeSe emotíons I'm feeliNG RiGHT Now

One THOUGHT, LimiTiNG Belief, OR HaBiT I WiLL LeT Go of is

WHere my ATTeNTioN GOes, eNeRGY flows, WHAT I focus on GROWS.

I WiLL emBRaCe THiS NeW THOUGHT, BeLief, OR HaBiT

I aSK my HeaRT aND THe UNiVeRSe TO GUiDe me.
TODaY, I am manifeSTiNG THiS (OR SOmeTHiNG BeTTeR)

NOW, I WiLL USe THe POWeR of my imaGiNaTiON TO ViSUaLiZe iT
COmiNG TRUe. FOR THRee miNUTeS, WiTH eyeS CLOSeD, I'LL
eXPeRieNCe HOW iT miGHT LOOK, feeL, SmeLL, TaSTe, aND SOUND
aS if iT iS HaPPeNiNG TODaY. I WiLL HaVe fUN DayDReamiNG
fReeLY aND WON'T GeT aTTaCHeD TO SPeCific OUTCOmeS.

NOTeS fROm my ViSUaLiZaTiON

TO KeeP my DReam aLiVe, I WiLL fOCUS ON THiS WORD
OR affiRmaTiON TODaY

ONe iNSPiReD aCTiON I WiLL TaKe iN THe DiReCTiON of my DReam iS

NOW, I SURReNDeR aNd TRUST. AND SO iT iS.

DAILY 👁 FOCUS

Date _____

Take THREE DEEP BREATHS.

IN THIS moment, I am GRATEFUL FOR

MiRACLES aND BLESSINGS I am CELEBRATING (EVEN ONES ON THE WAY)

I am PROUD of myself FOR

ONE THING I appRECiate aBOUT my BODY is

I acKNOWLEDGE THESE emotions I'm feeLING RIGHT NOW

ONE THOUGHT, LimiTING BELief, OR HaBiT I WILL LET GO of is

WHERE MY ATTENTION GOES, ENERGY flows, WHAT I focus on GROWS.

I WILL EMBRACE THIS NEW THOUGHT, BELIEF, OR HABIT

I ASK my HEART AND THE UNIVERSE TO GUIDE me.
TODAY, I AM manifESTING THIS (OR SOMETHING BETTER)

NOW, I WILL USE THE POWER of my imaGiNATION TO VISUALIZE iT
COMING TRUE. FOR THREE minutes, WITH eyes CLOSED, I'LL
EXPERIENCE HOW iT MIGHT LOOK, feel, SMELL, TASTE, AND SOUND
AS if iT iS HAPPENING TODAY. I WILL HAVE fUN DayDREAMING
fREELY AND WON'T GET ATTACHED TO SPECIFIC OUTCOMES.

NOTES fROM my VISUALIZATION

TO KEEP my DREAM ALIVE, I WILL fOCUS ON THIS WORD
OR affiRMATION TODAY

ONE INSPIRED ACTION I WILL TAKE IN THE DIRECTION of my DREAM iS

NOW, I SURRENDER and TRUST. AND SO iT iS.

DAILY  FOCUS

Date _____

Take THREE DEEP BREATHS.

IN THIS moment, I am GRATEFUL FOR

MiRacLes aND BLessiNGS I am CeLeBRatiNG (even ONes ON THe way)

I am PROUD of myseLf FOR

ONe THING I appReciate aBOUT my BODy is

I acKNOWLeDGe THese emOTiONS I'm feeLiNG RiGHT NOW

ONe THOUGHT, LimiTiNG BeLief, OR HaBiT I WiLL LeT GO of is

WHERE MY ATTENTION GOES, ENERGY flows, WHAT I focus on GROWS.

I WILL EMBRACE THIS NEW THOUGHT, BELIEF, OR HABIT

I ASK MY HEART AND THE UNIVERSE TO GUIDE ME.
TODAY, I AM MANIFESTING THIS (OR SOMETHING BETTER)

NOW, I WILL USE THE POWER OF MY IMAGINATION TO VISUALIZE IT
COMING TRUE. FOR THREE MINUTES, WITH EYES CLOSED, I'LL
EXPERIENCE HOW IT MIGHT LOOK, FEEL, SMELL, TASTE, AND SOUND
AS IF IT IS HAPPENING TODAY. I WILL HAVE FUN DAYDREAMING
FREELY AND WON'T GET ATTACHED TO SPECIFIC OUTCOMES.

NOTES FROM MY VISUALIZATION

TO KEEP MY DREAM ALIVE, I WILL FOCUS ON THIS WORD
OR AFFIRMATION TODAY

ONE INSPIRED ACTION I WILL TAKE IN THE DIRECTION OF MY DREAM IS

NOW, I SURRENDER and TRUST. AND SO IT IS.

DAILY 👁 FOCUS

Date _____

Take THREE DEEP BREATHS.

IN THIS moment, I am GRATEFUL FOR

MiRacLes and BLessinGs I am CeLeBRatinG (even ones on THe way)

I am PROUD of myself for

One THING I appreciate aBOUT my BODy is

I acknowledge these emotions I'm feeling RIGHT NOW

ONe THOUGHT, Limiting BeLief, OR HaBiT I WiLL LeT GO of is

WHERE MY ATTENTION GOES, ENERGY flows, WHAT I focus on GROWS.

I WILL EMBRACE THIS NEW THOUGHT, BELIEF, OR HABIT

I ASK my HEART AND THE UNIVERSE TO GUIDE me.
TODAY, I am manifesting THIS (OR SOMETHING BETTER)

NOW, I WILL USE THE POWER OF my imagination TO visualize iT
COming TRUE. FOR THREE minutes, WITH eyes CLOSED, I'LL
experience HOW iT might LOOK, feel, Smell, TASTE, AND SOUND
as if iT is HappeninG TODAY. I WILL HAVE fun DAYDREAMING
freely AND WON'T GET attached TO Specific OUTCOMES.

NOTES from my visualization

TO keep my DREAM aLive, I WILL focus ON THIS WORD
OR affirmation TODAY

ONE inSPIRED ACTION I WILL TAKE iN THE DIRECTION Of my DREAM is

NOW, I SURRENDER and TRUST. AND SO iT is.

DAILY 👁 FOCUS

Date _____

Take THREE DeeP BReaTHs.

In THis moment, I am GRaTeful foR

MiRacLes and BLessinGs I am CeLeBRaTinG (even ones on THe way)

I am PROUD of myself foR

One THinG I aPPReciaTe aBOUT my BODy is

I acKnowLeDGe THese emoTions I'm feeLinG RiGHT now

One THOUGHT, LimiTinG BeLief, oR HaBiT I wiLL LeT Go of is

WHERE MY ATTENTION GOES, ENERGY flows, WHAT I focus on GROWS.

I WILL EMBRACE THIS NEW THOUGHT, BELIEF, OR HABIT

I ASK my HEART AND THE UNIVERSE TO GUIDE me.
TODAY, I am manifesting THIS (OR SOMETHING BETTER)

NOW, I WILL USE THE POWER of my imaGINATION TO VISUALIZE iT
COMING TRUE. FOR THREE MINUTES, WITH eyes CLOSED, I'LL
EXPERIENCE HOW iT MIGHT LOOK, feeL, SMELL, TASTE, AND SOUND
AS iF iT iS HAPPENING TODAY. I WILL HAVE fUN DayDREAMING
fREELY AND WON'T GET ATTACHED TO SPECIFIC OUTCOMES.

NOTES fROM my VISUALIZATION

TO KEEP my DREAM ALIVE, I WILL fOCUS ON THIS WORD
OR affirmation TODAY

ONE INSPIRED ACTION I WILL TAKE IN THE DIRECTION of my DREAM iS

NOW, I SURRENDER and TRUST. AND SO iT iS.

DAILY 👁 FOCUS

Date _____

Take THREE DeeP BReaTHS.

In THiS moment, I am GRaTefuL foR

MiRacLes and BLessings I am CeLeBRaTing (even ones on THe way)

I am PROUD of myseLf foR

One THing I appReciaTe aBOUT my BODy is

I acKNOWLeDGe THese emOTiONS I'm feeLing RiGHT NOW

One THOUGHT, LimiTing BeLief, OR HaBiT I WiLL LeT GO of is

WHere MY ATTENTION GOes, eNERGY flows, WHAT I focus on GROWS.

I WiLL eMBRace THiS NeW THOUGHT, BeLief, OR HaBiT

I aSK MY HEART aND THe UNiVeRSe TO GUiDe Me.
TODay, I aM MaNifeSTiNG THiS (OR SOMeTHiNG BeTTeR)

NOW, I WiLL USe THe POWeR of MY iMaGiNaTiON TO visuaLize iT
COMiNG TRUe. FOR THRee MiNUTeS, WiTH eyeS CLOSeD, I'LL
exPeRieNCe HOW iT MiGHT LOOK, feeL, SMeLL, TaSTe, aND SOUND
aS if iT iS HaPPeNiNG TODay. I WiLL HaVe fUN DayDReaMiNG
fReeLy aND WON'T GeT aTTaCHeD TO SPeCific OUTCOMeS.

NOTeS fROM MY visuaLizaTiON

TO KeeP MY DReaM aLive, I WiLL fOCUS ON THiS WORD
OR affiRMaTiON TODay

ONe iNSPiReD aCTiON I WiLL TaKe iN THe DiReCTiON of MY DReaM iS

NOW, I SURReNDeR and TRUST. AND SO iT iS.

DAILY 👁 FOCUS

Date _____

Take THREE DEEP BREATHS.

In THIS moment, I am GRATEFUL foR

Miracles and Blessings I am Celebrating (even ones on the way)

I am PROUD of myself foR

One THING I appReciate aBout my BODy is

I acknowLedge THese emotions I'm feeling RIGHT NOW

One THOUGHT, Limiting Belief, oR HaBit I WiLL Let Go of is

WHERE MY ATTENTION GOES, ENERGY flows, WHAT I focus on GROWS.

I WILL EMBRACE THIS NEW THOUGHT, BELIEF, OR HABIT

I ASK my HEART AND THE UNIVERSE TO GUIDE me.
TODAY, I AM manifesTING THIS (OR SOMETHING BETTER)

NOW, I WILL USE THE POWER of my imaGinaTION TO visualize iT
COMING TRUE. FOR THREE minuTES, WITH eyes CLOSED, I'LL
EXPERIENCE HOW iT miGHT LOOK, feeL, SMELL, TASTE, AND SOUND
as if iT iS HAPPENING TODAY. I WILL HAVE fUN DAYDREAMING
fREELY AND WON'T GET aTTACHED TO SPECific OUTCOMES.

NOTES fROM my VISUALIZATION

TO KEEP my DREAM ALIVE, I WILL focUS ON THIS WORD
OR affiRMATION TODAY

ONE iNSPIRED ACTION I WILL TAKE IN THE DIRECTION of my DREAM iS

NOW, I SURRENDER and TRUST. AND SO iT iS.

DAILY  FOCUS

Date _____

Take three deep breaths.

In this moment, I am grateful for

Miracles and blessings I am celebrating (even ones on the way)

I am proud of myself for

One thing I appreciate about my body is

I acknowledge these emotions I'm feeling right now

One thought, limiting belief, or habit I will let go of is

WHERE MY ATTENTION GOES, ENERGY flows, WHAT I focus on GROWS.

I WILL EMBRACE THIS NEW THOUGHT, BELIEF, OR HABIT

I ASK MY HEART AND THE UNIVERSE TO GUIDE ME.
TODAY, I AM MANIFESTING THIS (OR SOMETHING BETTER)

NOW, I WILL USE THE POWER OF MY IMAGINATION TO VISUALIZE IT
COMING TRUE. FOR THREE MINUTES, WITH EYES CLOSED, I'LL
EXPERIENCE HOW IT MIGHT LOOK, FEEL, SMELL, TASTE, AND SOUND
AS IF IT IS HAPPENING TODAY. I WILL HAVE FUN DAYDREAMING
FREELY AND WON'T GET ATTACHED TO SPECIFIC OUTCOMES.

NOTES FROM MY VISUALIZATION

TO KEEP MY DREAM ALIVE, I WILL FOCUS ON THIS WORD
OR AFFIRMATION TODAY

ONE INSPIRED ACTION I WILL TAKE IN THE DIRECTION OF MY DREAM IS

NOW, I SURRENDER and TRUST. AND SO IT IS.

DAILY  FOCUS

Date _____

Take THREE Deep BReaTHs.

In THis moment, I am GRaTeful foR

MiRacles and BLessinGs I am celeBRaTinG (even ones on THe way)

I am PROUD of myself foR

One THInG I appReciaTe aBouT my BoDy is

I acknowledGe THese emoTions I'm feelinG RiGHT now

One THOUGHT, LimiTinG BeLief, oR HaBiT I will leT Go of is

WHERE MY ATTENTION GOES, ENERGY flows, WHAT I focus on GROWS.

I WILL EMBRACE THIS NEW THOUGHT, BELIEF, OR HABIT

I ASK MY HEART AND THE UNIVERSE TO GUIDE ME.
TODAY, I AM MANIFESTING THIS (OR SOMETHING BETTER)

NOW, I WILL USE THE POWER OF MY IMAGINATION TO VISUALIZE IT
COMING TRUE. FOR THREE MINUTES, WITH EYES CLOSED, I'LL
EXPERIENCE HOW IT MIGHT LOOK, FEEL, SMELL, TASTE, AND SOUND
AS IF IT IS HAPPENING TODAY. I WILL HAVE FUN DAYDREAMING
FREELY AND WON'T GET ATTACHED TO SPECIFIC OUTCOMES.

NOTES FROM MY VISUALIZATION

TO KEEP MY DREAM ALIVE, I WILL FOCUS ON THIS WORD
OR AFFIRMATION TODAY

ONE INSPIRED ACTION I WILL TAKE IN THE DIRECTION OF MY DREAM IS

NOW, I SURRENDER and TRUST. AND SO IT IS.

DAiLY 👁 FOCUS

Date _____

Take THREE DEEP BREaTHS.

IN THiS moment, I am GRaTEfUL foR

MiRaCLES aND BLESSiNGS I am CELEBRaTiNG (EVEN ONES ON THE WaY)

I am PROUD of myself foR

ONE THiNG I aPPRECiaTE aBOUT my BODy is

I aCKNOWLEDGE THESE EmoTiONS I'm fEELiNG RiGHT NOW

ONE THOUGHT, LimiTiNG BELiEf, OR HaBiT I WiLL LET GO of is

WHERE MY ATTENTION GOES, ENERGY flows, WHAT I focus on GROWS.

I WILL EMBRACE THIS NEW THOUGHT, BELIEF, OR HABIT

I ASK my HEART AND THE UNIVERSE TO GUIDE me.
TODAY, I am manifesting THIS (OR SOMETHING BETTER)

NOW, I WILL USE THE POWER of my imagination TO VISUALIZE iT
COMING TRUE. FOR THREE minutes, WITH eyes CLOSED, I'LL
EXPERIENCE HOW iT miGHT LOOK, feel, SMELL, TASTE, AND SOUND
AS iF iT iS HAPPENING TODAY. I WILL HAVE fUN DayDREAMING
FREELY AND WON'T GET ATTACHED TO SPECIFIC OUTCOMES.

NOTES fROM my VISUALIZATION

TO KEEP my DREAM ALIVE, I WILL fOCUS ON THIS WORD
OR affirmation TODAY

ONE INSPIRED ACTION I WILL TAKE IN THE DIRECTION of my DREAM iS

NOW, I SURRENDER and TRUST. AND SO iT iS.

DAILY 👁 FOCUS

Date _____

Take THREE DeeP BReatHS.

In THiS moment, I am GRatefUL foR

MiRacLeS anD BLeSSinGS I am CeLeBRatinG (even oneS on THe way)

I am PROUD of myself foR

One THinG I appReciate aBOUT my BODy iS

I acknowLeDGe THeSe emotionS I'm feeLinG RiGHT now

One THOUGHT, Limiting BeLief, oR HaBiT I WiLL Let Go of iS

WHere MY ATTENTiON GOes, eNeRGY flows, WHAT I focus on GROWS.

I WiLL emBRaCe THiS New THOUGHT, BeLief, OR HaBiT

I aSK my HeaRT aND THe UNiVeRSe TO GUiDe me.
TODay, I am manifeSTiNG THiS (OR SOmeTHiNG BeTTeR)

NOW, I WiLL USe THe POWeR of my imaGiNaTiON TO ViSUaLiZe iT
COmiNG TRUe. FOR THRee minUTeS, WiTH eyeS CLOSeD, I'LL
eXPeRieNCe HOW iT miGHT LOOK, feeL, SmeLL, TaSTe, aND SOUND
aS if iT iS HaPPeNiNG TODay. I WiLL HaVe fUN DayDReamiNG
fReeLy aND WON'T GeT aTTaCHeD TO SPeCific OUTCOmeS.

NOTeS fROm my ViSUaLiZaTiON

TO KeeP my DReam aLiVe, I WiLL fOCUS ON THiS WORD
OR affiRmaTiON TODay

ONe iNSPiReD aCTiON I WiLL TaKe iN THe DiReCTiON of my DReam iS

NOW, I SURReNDer aND TRUST. aND SO iT iS.

DAiLY  FOCUS

Date _____

Take THRee Deep BReaTHS.

In THiS moment, I am GRateful foR

Miracles and BLessinGS I am celeBRatinG (even ones on THe way)

I am PROUD of myself foR

One THinG I appReciate aBouT my BoDy is

I acknowleDGe THese emotions I'm feelinG RiGHT now

One THOUGHT, LimitinG Belief, oR HaBit I will let Go of is

WHere MY ATTeNTioN Goes, eNeRGY flows, WHAT I focus on GROWS.

I WiLL eMBRaCe THiS NeW THOUGHT, Belief, OR HaBiT

I aSK My HeaRT aND THe UNiVeRSe TO GUiDe me.
TODay, I aM maNifeSTiNG THiS (OR SOmeTHiNG BeTTeR)

NOW, I WiLL USe THe POWeR of My imaGiNaTiON TO ViSUaLize iT
COmiNG TRUe. FOR THRee miNUTeS, WiTH eyeS CLOSeD, I'LL
exPeRieNCe HOW iT miGHT LOOK, feeL, SmeLL, TaSTe, aND SOUND
aS if iT iS HaPPeNiNG TODay. I WiLL HaVe fUN DayDReamiNG
fReeLy aND WON'T GeT aTTaCHeD TO SPeCific oUTComeS.

NOTeS fROM My ViSUaLizaTiON

TO KeeP My DReam aLiVe, I WiLL foCUS ON THiS WORD
OR affiRmaTiON TODay

ONe iNSPiReD aCTiON I WiLL TaKe iN THe DiReCTiON of My DReam iS

NOW, I SURReNDer aND TRUST. AND SO iT iS.

DAILY 👁 FOCUS

Date _____

Take THREE DeeP BReaTHS.

IN THiS moment, I am GRaTefuL foR

MiRacLeS aND BLeSSiNGS I am CeLeBRaTiNG (eVeN oNeS oN THe way)

I am PROUD of myseLf foR

oNe THiNG I aPPReciaTe aBoUT my BoDy is

I acKNowLeDGe THeSe emoTioNS I'm feeLiNG RiGHT Now

oNe THoUGHT, LimiTiNG BeLief, oR HaBiT I wiLL LeT Go of is

WHere MY ATTeNTioN Goes, eNeRGY flows, WHAT I focus on GROWS.

I WiLL emBRaCe THiS NeW THOUGHT, BeLief, OR HaBiT

I aSK my HeaRT AND THe UNiVeRSe TO GUiDe me.
TODay, I am manifeSTiNG THiS (OR SOmeTHiNG BeTTeR)

NoW, I WiLL USe THe POWeR of my imaGiNaTiON TO ViSUaLiZe iT
COminG TRUe. FOR THRee minUTeS, WiTH eyeS CLOSeD, I'LL
exPeRieNCe HOW iT miGHT LOOK, feeL, SmeLL, TaSTe, AND SOUND
aS if iT iS HaPPeNiNG TODay. I WiLL HaVe fUN DayDReaminG
fReeLy AND WON'T GeT aTTaCHeD TO SpeCific OUTComeS.

NOTeS fROm my ViSUaLiZaTiON

TO KeeP my DReam aLive, I WiLL focUS ON THiS WORD
OR affiRmaTiON TODay

ONe iNSPiReD aCTiON I WiLL TaKe iN THe DiReCTiON of my DReam iS

NOW, I SURReNDeR and TRUST. AND SO iT iS.

DAILY 👁 FOCUS

Date _____

Take THREE Deep BReaTHS.

In THis moment, I am GRaTeFuL foR

MiRaCLes anD BLessinGs I am CeLeBRaTinG (even ones on THe way)

I am PROuD of myseLf foR

One THinG I appReCiaTe aBOUT my BODy is

I aCKnowLeDGe THese emoTions I'm feeLinG RiGHT now

One THOUGHT, LimiTinG BeLief, oR HaBiT I wiLL LeT Go of is

WHERE MY ATTENTION GOES, ENERGY flows, WHAT I focus on GROWS.

I WILL EMBRACE THIS NEW THOUGHT, BELIEF, OR HABIT

I ASK MY HEART AND THE UNIVERSE TO GUIDE ME.
TODAY, I AM MANIFESTING THIS (OR SOMETHING BETTER)

NOW, I WILL USE THE POWER OF MY IMAGINATION TO VISUALIZE IT
COMING TRUE. FOR THREE MINUTES, WITH EYES CLOSED, I'LL
EXPERIENCE HOW IT MIGHT LOOK, FEEL, SMELL, TASTE, AND SOUND
AS IF IT IS HAPPENING TODAY. I WILL HAVE FUN DAYDREAMING
FREELY AND WON'T GET ATTACHED TO SPECIFIC OUTCOMES.

NOTES FROM MY VISUALIZATION

TO KEEP MY DREAM ALIVE, I WILL FOCUS ON THIS WORD
OR AFFIRMATION TODAY

ONE INSPIRED ACTION I WILL TAKE IN THE DIRECTION OF MY DREAM IS

NOW, I SURRENDER and TRUST. AND SO IT IS.

DAILY 👁 FOCUS

Date _____

Take THREE DEEP BREATHS.

In THIS moment, I am GRATEFUL for

MiRacLes and BLeSSiNGS I am CeLeBRATiNG (even ones on THE way)

I am PROUD of myseLf for

One THiNG I appReciaTe aBOUT my BODy is

I acKNOWLEDGe THese emoTions I'm feeLiNG RiGHT NOW

One THOUGHT, LimiTiNG BeLief, OR HaBiT I WiLL Let GO of is

WHERE MY ATTENTION GOES, ENERGY flows, WHAT I focus on GROWS.

I WILL EMBRACE THIS NEW THOUGHT, BELIEF, OR HABIT

I ASK my HEART AND THE UNIVERSE TO GUIDE me.
TODAY, I am manifesting THIS (OR something BETTER)

NOW, I WILL USE THE POWER of my imagination TO visualize iT
COMING TRUE. FOR THREE minutes, WITH eyes CLOSED, I'LL
EXPERIENCE HOW iT miGHT LOOK, feel, smell, TASTE, AND SOUND
AS iF iT iS HAPPENING TODAY. I WILL HAVE fUN DAYDREAMING
FREELY AND WON'T GET ATTACHED TO SPECIFIC OUTCOMES.

NOTES FROM my VISUALIZATION

TO KEEP my DREAM alive, I WILL focus ON THIS WORD
OR affirmation TODAY

ONE INSPIRED ACTION I WILL TAKE IN THE DIRECTION of my DREAM iS

NOW, I SURRENDER and TRUST. AND SO iT iS.

DAILY  FOCUS

Date _____

Take THREE Deep BREaTHs.

In THis moment, I am GRaTeful foR

Miracles and Blessings I am Celebrating (even ones on the way)

I am PROUD of myself foR

One THING I appReciaTe aBOUT my BODY is

I acknowLeDGe These emotions I'm feeling RiGHT now

One THOUGHT, Limiting Belief, OR HaBiT I wiLL LeT GO of is

WHERE MY ATTENTION GOES, ENERGY flows, WHAT I focus on GROWS.

I WILL EMBRACE THIS NEW THOUGHT, BELIEF, OR HABIT

I ASK MY HEART AND THE UNIVERSE TO GUIDE ME.
TODAY, I AM MANIFESTING THIS (OR SOMETHING BETTER)

NOW, I WILL USE THE POWER OF MY IMAGINATION TO VISUALIZE IT
COMING TRUE. FOR THREE MINUTES, WITH EYES CLOSED, I'LL
EXPERIENCE HOW IT MIGHT LOOK, FEEL, SMELL, TASTE, AND SOUND
AS IF IT IS HAPPENING TODAY. I WILL HAVE FUN DAYDREAMING
FREELY AND WON'T GET ATTACHED TO SPECIFIC OUTCOMES.

NOTES FROM MY VISUALIZATION

TO KEEP MY DREAM ALIVE, I WILL FOCUS ON THIS WORD
OR AFFIRMATION TODAY

ONE INSPIRED ACTION I WILL TAKE IN THE DIRECTION OF MY DREAM IS

NOW, I SURRENDER and TRUST. AND SO IT IS.

DAiLY 👁 FOCUS

Date _____

Take THRee Deep BReaTHs.

In THis moment, I am GRaTeFuL FoR

MiRacLes and BLessiNGs I am CeLeBRaTiNG (even ones on THe way)

I am PROUD of myseLF FoR

One THiNG I aPPReciaTe aBOUT my BODy is

I acKNOWLeDGe THese emoTiONs I'm FeeLiNG RiGHT NOW

One THOUGHT, LimiTiNG BeLief, OR HaBiT I WiLL LeT GO of is

WHERE MY ATTENTION GOES, ENERGY flows, WHAT I focus on GROWS.

I WILL EMBRACE THIS NEW THOUGHT, BELIEF, OR HABIT

I ASK MY HEART AND THE UNIVERSE TO GUIDE ME.
TODAY, I AM MANIFESTING THIS (OR SOMETHING BETTER)

NOW, I WILL USE THE POWER OF MY IMAGINATION TO VISUALIZE IT
COMING TRUE. FOR THREE MINUTES, WITH EYES CLOSED, I'LL
EXPERIENCE HOW IT MIGHT LOOK, FEEL, SMELL, TASTE, AND SOUND
AS IF IT IS HAPPENING TODAY. I WILL HAVE FUN DAYDREAMING
FREELY AND WON'T GET ATTACHED TO SPECIFIC OUTCOMES.

NOTES FROM MY VISUALIZATION

TO KEEP MY DREAM ALIVE, I WILL FOCUS ON THIS WORD
OR AFFIRMATION TODAY

ONE INSPIRED ACTION I WILL TAKE IN THE DIRECTION OF MY DREAM IS

NOW, I SURRENDER and TRUST. AND SO IT IS.

DAILY 👁 FOCUS

Date _____

Take THREE DEEP BREATHS.

IN THIS moment, I am GRATEFUL FOR

Miracles and BLESSINGS I am celeBRATING (even ones on the way)

I am PROUD of myself FOR

ONE THING I appreciate aBOUT my BODY is

I ackNOWLEDGE THESE emoTIONS I'm feeLING RIGHT NOW

ONE THOUGHT, LimiTING BeLief, OR HaBiT I WILL LET GO of is

WHERE MY ATTENTION GOES, ENERGY flows, WHAT I focus on GROWS.

I WILL EMBRACE THIS NEW THOUGHT, BELIEF, OR HABIT

I ASK my HEART AND THE UNIVERSE TO GUIDE me.
TODAY, I AM MANIFESTING THIS (OR SOMETHING BETTER)

NOW, I WILL USE THE POWER of my IMAGINATION TO VISUALIZE IT
COMING TRUE. FOR THREE MINUTES, WITH eyes CLOSED, I'LL
EXPERIENCE HOW IT MIGHT LOOK, feel, SMELL, TASTE, AND SOUND
AS IF IT IS HAPPENING TODAY. I WILL HAVE FUN DAYDREAMING
FREELY AND WON'T GET ATTACHED TO SPECIFIC OUTCOMES.

NOTES FROM my VISUALIZATION

TO KEEP my DREAM ALIVE, I WILL FOCUS ON THIS WORD
OR affirmation TODAY

ONE INSPIRED ACTION I WILL TAKE IN THE DIRECTION of my DREAM IS

NOW, I SURRENDER and TRUST. AND SO IT IS.

DAiLY  FOCUS

Date _____

Take THRee DeeP BReaTHS.

In THiS moment, I am GRaTeFuL foR

MiRacLeS anD BLeSSinGS I am CeLeBRaTinG (even oneS on THe way)

I am PROUD of myseLf foR

One THinG I aPPReciaTe aBOUT my BODy iS

I acKnowLeDGe THese emoTionS I'm feeLinG RiGHT now

One THOUGHT, LimiTinG BeLief, OR HaBiT I wiLL LeT Go of iS

WHERE MY ATTENTION GOES, ENERGY flows, WHAT I focus on GROWS.

I WILL EMBRACE THIS NEW THOUGHT, BELIEF, OR HABIT

I ASK my HEART AND THE UNIVERSE TO GUIDE me.
TODAY, I AM MANIFESTING THIS (OR SOMETHING BETTER)

NOW, I WILL USE THE POWER OF my IMAGINATION TO VISUALIZE IT
COMING TRUE. FOR THREE MINUTES, WITH eyes CLOSED, I'LL
EXPERIENCE HOW IT MIGHT LOOK, feel, SMELL, TASTE, AND SOUND
AS IF IT IS HAPPENING TODAY. I WILL HAVE fUN DAYDREAMING
fREELY AND WON'T GET ATTACHED TO SPECIFIC OUTCOMES.

NOTES fROM my VISUALIZATION

TO KEEP my DREAM ALIVE, I WILL fOCUS ON THIS WORD
OR affiRMATION TODAY

ONE INSPIRED ACTION I WILL TAKE IN THE DIRECTION OF my DREAM IS

NOW, I SURRENDER and TRUST. AND SO IT IS.

DAILY  FOCUS

Date _____

Take THREE Deep BReaTHS.

IN THis moment, I am GRaTeful foR

MiRacLes aND BLessiNGS I am celeBRaTiNG (eveN oNes oN THe way)

I am PROUD of myself foR

oNe THiNG I appReciaTe aBOUT my BODy is

I acKNowLeDGe THese emoTioNS I'm feeliNG RiGHT Now

oNe THOUGHT, LimiTiNG Belief, oR HaBiT I wiLL LeT Go of is

WHere my ATTeNTioN Goes, eNeRGY flows, WHaT I focus on GROWS.

I WiLL emBRaCe THiS NeW THOUGHT, BeLief, OR HaBiT

I aSK my HeaRT aND THe UNiVeRSe TO GUiDe me.
TODay, I am maNifeSTiNG THiS (OR SOmeTHiNG BeTTeR)

NOW, I WiLL USe THe POWeR of my imaGiNaTioN TO ViSUaLiZe iT
COmiNG TRUe. FOR THRee miNUTeS, WiTH eyeS CLOSeD, I'LL
eXPeRieNCe HOW iT miGHT LOOK, feeL, SmeLL, TaSTe, aND SOUND
aS if iT iS HaPPeNiNG TODay. I WiLL HaVe fUN DayDReamiNG
fReeLy aND WON'T GeT aTTaCHeD TO SPeCifiC OUTCOmeS.
NOTeS fROm my ViSUaLiZaTioN

TO KeeP my DReam aLiVe, I WiLL foCUS ON THiS WORD
OR affiRmaTioN TODay

ONe iNSPiReD aCTioN I WiLL TaKe iN THe DiReCTioN of my DReam iS

NOW, I SURReNDeR aND TRUST. aND SO iT iS.

DAILY  FOCUS

Date _____

Take THREE Deep BReaTHS.

IN THiS moment, I am GRaTeFUL foR

MiRacLes aND BLeSSiNGS I am CeLeBRaTiNG (even ONes ON THe way)

I am PROUD of myseLf foR

ONe THING I appReciaTe aBOUT my BODy is

I acKNOWLeDGe THese emoTiONS I'm feeLiNG RiGHT NOW

ONe THOUGHT, LimiTiNG BeLief, OR HaBiT I WiLL LeT GO of is

WHERE MY ATTENTION GOES, ENERGY flows, WHAT I focus on GROWS.

I WILL EMBRACE THIS NEW THOUGHT, BELIEF, OR HABIT

I ASK MY HEART AND THE UNIVERSE TO GUIDE ME.
TODAY, I AM MANIFESTING THIS (OR SOMETHING BETTER)

NOW, I WILL USE THE POWER OF MY IMAGINATION TO VISUALIZE IT
COMING TRUE. FOR THREE MINUTES, WITH EYES CLOSED, I'LL
EXPERIENCE HOW IT MIGHT LOOK, FEEL, SMELL, TASTE, AND SOUND
AS IF IT IS HAPPENING TODAY. I WILL HAVE FUN DAYDREAMING
FREELY AND WON'T GET ATTACHED TO SPECIFIC OUTCOMES.

NOTES FROM MY VISUALIZATION

TO KEEP MY DREAM ALIVE, I WILL FOCUS ON THIS WORD
OR AFFIRMATION TODAY

ONE INSPIRED ACTION I WILL TAKE IN THE DIRECTION OF MY DREAM IS

NOW, I SURRENDER AND TRUST. AND SO IT IS.

DAILY 👁 FOCUS

Date _____

Take THREE DeeP BReaTHs.

In THIS moment, I am GRATeful foR

MiRacLes anD BLessinGs I am CeLeBRatinG (even ones on THe way)

I am PROUD of myself foR

One THinG I appReciate aBout my BoDy is

I acknowLeDGe THese emotions I'm feelinG RiGHT now

One THOUGHT, LimitinG BeLief, oR HaBit I wiLL Let Go of is

WHere MY ATTeNTiON GOes, eNerGY flows, WHaT I focus on GROWS.

I WiLL eMBRaCe THiS NeW THOUGHT, BeLief, OR HaBiT

I aSK My HeaRT aND THe UNiVeRSe TO GUiDe Me.
TODaY, I aM maNifeSTiNG THiS (OR SOMeTHiNG BeTTeR)

NOW, I WiLL USe THe POWeR of My imaGiNaTiON TO ViSUaLize iT COMiNG TRUe. FOR THRee MiNUTeS, WiTH eyes CLOSeD, I'LL eXPeRieNCe HOW iT MiGHT LOOK, feel, SMeLL, TaSTe, aND SOUND aS if iT iS HaPPeNiNG TODaY. I WiLL HaVe fUN DayDReaMiNG fReeLy aND WON'T GeT aTTaCHeD TO SPeCific OUTCOMes.

NOTeS fROM My ViSUaLizaTiON

TO Keep My DReaM aLive, I WiLL focUS ON THiS WORD
OR affiRMaTiON TODaY

ONe iNSPiReD aCTiON I WiLL TaKe iN THe DiReCTiON of My DReaM iS

NOW, I SURReNDer aND TRUST. aND SO iT iS.

DAiLY 👁 FOCUS

Date _____

Take THRee DeeP BReaTHS.

IN THiS moment, I am GRaTefuL foR

MiRacLeS aND BLeSSiNGS I am CeLeBRaTiNG (eveN oNeS oN THe way)

I am PROUD of myseLf foR

oNe THiNG I aPPReCiaTe aBouT my BoDy iS

I acKNowLeDGe THeSe emoTioNS I'm feeLiNG RiGHT Now

oNe THOUGHT, LimiTiNG BeLief, oR HaBiT I wiLL LeT Go of iS

WHere my ATTentioN Goes, eNeRGY flows, WHaT I focus on GROWS.

I WiLL eMBRace THIS NeW THOUGHT, BeLief, OR HaBiT

I aSK my HEaRT aND THe UNiveRSe TO GUiDe me.
TODay, I am manifeSTiNG THIS (OR SOmeTHiNG BeTTeR)

NOW, I WiLL USe THe POWeR of my imaGiNaTioN TO viSUaLize iT
COmiNG TRUe. FOR THRee minUTeS, WiTH eyeS CLOSeD, I'LL
exPeRieNCe HOW iT miGHT LOOK, feeL, SmeLL, TaSTe, aND SOUND
aS if iT iS HaPPeNiNG TODay. I WiLL Have fUN DayDReamiNG
fReeLy aND WON'T GeT aTTaCHeD TO SPeCific OUTComeS.

NOTeS fROm my viSUaLizaTioN

TO KeeP my DReam aLive, I WiLL focUS ON THIS WORD
OR affiRmaTion TODay

ONe iNSPiReD aCTioN I WiLL TaKe iN THe DiReCTioN of my DReam iS

NOW, I SURReNDeR and TRUST. AND SO iT iS.

MOON MaGiC

Use these pages to write, draw, or paint about
your moon ritual and what you experience.

NeW MOON RiTUAL

Date _____

FULL MOON RiTUAL

Date _____

90-DAY CHECK-IN

Reflect

WHAT HAS BEEN THE BIGGEST IMPACT OF THIS PRACTICE FOR ME?

WHAT HAVE I LEARNED ABOUT MYSELF AND MY DESIRES?

WHAT DID MY HEART AND THE UNIVERSE TEACH ME?

CLEAR and RELEASE

ARE THERE ANY CONSISTENT, BROADER LIMITING BELIEFS, DOUBTS, OR FEARS THAT SHOWED UP DURING THIS PRACTICE THAT I CAN CONTINUE TO HEAL?

NOW THAT I'VE COMPLETED THIS 90-DAY PRACTICE, WHAT ELSE AM I READY TO LET GO OF?

HOW WILL I CONTINUE TO SUPPORT MYSELF IN HEALING AND INTEGRATING MY SHADOW, SUCH AS LIMITING BELIEFS, BLOCKED EMOTIONS, AND SELF—SABOTAGING PATTERNS?

Celebrate

In the last 90 days, what are some beautiful moments, blessings, and manifestations that have occurred?

What major aspects of my life am I most grateful for and proud of?

What do I love most about myself?
What do I love most about my body?

Create

What new possibilities, dreams, and desires have opened to me over the last 90 days?

How will I continue moving toward these dreams?

What will I do to continue practicing my favorite aspects of this ritual?

RITUALS

⚡ CREATE MY OWN DAILY PRACTICE

✳ WALK IN NATURE

♡ LIE on EARTH or STAND BAREFOOT

✳ SWIM IN NATURAL WATERS

♡ ECSTATICALLY DANCE or SHAKE!

⚡ NAP WHEN NUDGED to

♡ MEDITATE ♡ BREATHWORK

✳ YOGA, QIGONG, MASSAGE, and other BODYWORK

♡ LISTEN to or PLAY MUSIC

♡ SPEND more TIME WITH PEOPLE WHO REMIND me of MY MAGIC

WAYS I CAN CONTINUE to WATER the flowers IN MY GARDEN through CONSCIOUS fOCUS...

I AM the Love, Peace, and JOY that I Seek.

♥ ENJOY Live music
⚡ TRaveL and EXPLore
❀ Keep a DReAM DiarY
♡ LeaRN to MAKe SOMETHING NeW
⚡ VOLUNTeer or SERVE others
✳ CReaTe or JoiN a Sacred SUPPORTiVE CiRCLE
♡ DO SOMETHING BRaVE or SPONTaNeOUS
❀ EXPLore, CONNeCT WiTH, and HeaL my LiNeaGe

❀ PAINT, DRaW, COLor!
♡ ReCiTe MaNTRaS or AFFIRMaTiONS
⚡ GeT SUPPORT from a therapist, shaman, COaCH or other GUiDe
♡ MaKe a WReaTH, BOUQUeT, or EaRTH ALTar
❀ DO WHAT I LOVeD to DO as a KiD
⚡ JOURNaL: TRY AUTOMaTiC WRiTiNG

♡ DO MORe of WHATever MAKeS Me Come ALiVe!

GeT CuRiOuS

Name your weeds. Where do you still feel blocked, stuck, unlovable, or small? What keeps popping up?

Dig Deeper. What are these buried emotions or fears? Where do you feel it in your body?

GENTLY EXPLORE THE WEEDS IN YOUR ENERGETIC GARDEN. THE MORE YOU LOVE THE PARTS OF YOURSELF THAT YOU AVOID, THE GREATER THE BREAKTHROUGHS YOU WILL ACHIEVE.

Use the columns below to name the fears, doubts, guilt, shame, or other shadow aspects you may have noticed over 90 days.

GET AT THE ROOT. WHERE DID THIS COME FROM? IS THIS SOMETHING YOU INHERITED, LEARNED, OR ARE CARRYING FROM A PAST EXPERIENCE?

LET IT GO. IS IT TRUE? CAN YOU LEAVE IT THERE BUT STOP WATERING IT? LIST SOME COUNTERPOINTS OR SOLUTIONS.

CELEBRATE YOUR Life!

YOUR GARDEN CONTAINS BEAUTY AND WONDER.
EMBRACE EVERYTHING YOU'VE CULTIVATED, AND
DELIGHT IN THE THINGS YOU LOVE ABOUT YOUR
LIFE, YOUR BODY, AND YOUR BLESSINGS.

List favorite words or affirmations. Illustrate miracles, blessings, and manifestations that have occurred. Add ideas for nourishing the positive growth in your life.

CREATE YOUR FUTURE!

By NURTURING a DEEPER RELATIONSHIP WITH your HEART AND THE UNIVERSE, THE SEEDS you HAVE PLANTED ALONG THIS JOURNEY WILL FLOWER AND BEAR FRUIT LONG INTO THE FUTURE.

Add words or images that represent your heart's biggest, boldest yearnings and what you're being guided to create in your life.

Kimothy Joy is a Maine-based artist, writer, mother, meditator, modern mystic, and female-empowerment advocate. She believes in the infinite potential of every person and that we're spiritual beings having a human experience here—might as well make it an awesome one!

Her signature style combines watercolor with hand-lettering and highlights nourishing, uplifting messages.

Kimothy's artwork appeared around the world following the 2017 Women's March on Washington, and she has since collaborated with Amanda Gorman for She's the First, the U.S. Women's National Soccer Team, GUCCI, Hello Sunshine, MAKERS, Cleo Wade, Hope Smith, and many others. Her work has been featured in the *Huffington Post, Teen Vogue, Vogue,* Refinery29, *Glamour,* the *Washington Post,* and more.

She is the author and illustrator of *That's What She Said: Wise Words from Influential Women* and the *Focus Pocus* and *Grow with the Flow* calendars. Her next book celebrates female friendship and debuts in February 2024.

Learn more at kimothyjoy.com and connect with her on Instagram @kimothy.joy.